WHEN ALL ELSE FAILS

WHEN ALL ELSE FAILS

Christian Arguments on Violent Revolution

Edited by IDO-C

Pilgrim Press
Philadelphia   Boston

SBN 8298-0187-1
Library of Congress Catalog Card Number 74-131205

Copyright © 1970 United Church Press
Philadelphia, Pennsylvania

Based on the book published originally in Milan, Italy as *Vangelo Violenza Rivoluzione.*
© Arnoldo Mondadori Editore 1969. I edizione marzo 1969. Documentinuovi.

The publisher is grateful to the organizations that granted permission to have their materials translated into English or reprinted.
Heinz Dietrich Wendland (chapter 1) and Vitaly Borovoj (chapter 4) wrote for the conference on "Church and Society" in Geneva. Used by permission of the World Council of Churches.
Almeri Bezerra de Melo (chapter 2), José Maria Gonzalez-Ruiz (chapter 5), and P. L. Geschiere and H. G. Schulte Nordholt (chapter 7) wrote for the *IDO-C Bulletin.* Chapter 9 was also written for the *IDO-C Bulletin.*
"A Theological Perspective on Human Liberation" by Richard Shaull (chapter 3) is reprinted by courtesy of the CICOP Conference on the U.S. Bishops' Committee for Latin America.
Paul Blanquart (chapter 6) and Albert Paul Lentin (chapter 8) wrote for a conference organized by *La Lettre* and *IDO-C.* The original articles appeared in the *IDO-C Bulletin* and have been included in a book published by *La Lettre.*

IDO-C International Series SBN 8298-0185-5

CONTENTS

WHEN ALL ELSE FAILS

INTRODUCTION TO
AMERICAN EDITION

When All Else Fails presents the compositions, languages, and interactions of revolution. Its chapters form a comprehensive, worldwide gathering of perspectives that seek to define and depict the principal forces of our time that flaunt the label "revolution."

As several chapters demonstrate, a fundamental reality of contemporary politics is the diversity, scope, and intensity of revolutions and revolutionary forces throughout the so-called Third World—that broad, somewhat ambiguous label that is now used to depict the peoples, nations, and movements of Asia, Africa, and Latin and South America. Over half the material in this book comes from Third World authors, documents, and experiences. As such the book is a text of primary resources and studies depicting the revolutionary forces which polarize much of the world. Here are to be found prognostications and intelligent speculations regarding the fate of history and humanity. At the same time, both individually and as a whole, these chapters can be read as an exercise in practical politics. They address the root dilemma of all politics, the relationship of institutions to the social order. Specifically, the ancient social institution of the Church is examined in the light of revolutionary forces, violence, and radical breaks with existing social orders.

Part I attempts to address the complex theoretical and ideological issues in the relationships of the Church and revolutions.

Parameters for an immense variety of issues are depicted in responses to the basic question, "Can a Christian be a revolutionary?"

German theologian Heinz Dietrich Wendland develops a historical perspective of the principal concepts of revolution and how these are related to Christians. He finds present-day civilization in a situation of "total revolution," a phenomenon born in technical and scientific developments, which are all-pervasive or "total" in their extent, intensity, and force upon society. While from a historical viewpoint Christianity has often ignored revolutionary movements, Wendland finds that the present will not permit Christians to avoid the realities and implication of revolutions. He concludes that the authentic, viable revolution bases itself upon history and introduces a new social order into history.

Brazilian sociologist Almeri Bezerra de Melo examines revolutions and violence from a viewpoint of history and contemporary Latin American politics. The basic question is the quest for economic liberation. De Melo demonstrates that there must be more than a verbal distinction between revolution and violence. In making his case, he reviews the Church's involved role in violent actions throughout history. While at best it is an ambiguous history, it is still unquestionably clear that often and in a wide variety of situations, Christians have utilized violent action. The crux of this history is the Church's persistence in making distinctions between the violence of the poor and that of the rich. The Church has demonstrated often an affinity for and baptism of the violence of the rich. The accompanying "control" of the poor (including superficial promises of eschatological deliverance) raises fundamental questions concerning the Church's motives and role in society.

U.S. theologian Richard Shaull confronts the churches with more data similar to that presented by de Melo. The Church's theologies should, in Shaull's view, acknowledge a basic truth of political reality: that the liberation of people can and will upset existing social systems and sometimes this will demand violent actions. The crucial question for society's institutions (including the churches) is whether the old can make way for the new without violence. Shaull proposes a simple but direct and forceful method for comprehending revolutions: the old is so often wrong simply because it blocks and denies justice and human welfare. The political fruition of this denial and obstruction is increasingly that of violent wars for national liberation. In this milieu, the Church's fate is governed by where it decides to stand and with whom it associates.

The question of the Church's fate in times of revolution is eloquently evaluated by the Orthodox Metropolitan of Leningrad, The Most Rev. Vitaly Borovoj. He speaks of the Gospels as showing a God who revolutionizes history and concludes that theology needs to put itself into the service of social revolutions. In poignant understatement, the Metropolitan suggests that Western Christians have much to learn from the experiences of the Russian Christians, including the consequences of resistance to a new order. His fundamental principle is that Christians ought to associate with movements that seek social justice. The fate of the churches is tied to their stance vis-à-vis the revolutionary movements of an age. And in this stance it is possible to discover an identity with the "revolutionary gospels."

Part II presents three models for interpreting the types, forms, and processes of revolutions. Spanish biblical scholar J. M. Gonzalez-Ruiz explores the potentialities for Christianity and a scientific (non-Marxist) socialism. For Gonzalez-Ruiz, there is an irreconcilable clash between the gospel and capitalism and thus Christians are urged to consider themselves as aliens in any capitalist society. The proffered alternative is a scientific socialism that embodies building social structures in which exploitation of persons or classes is prevented and resisted.

French Christian and Marxist theoretician Paul Blanquart turns his attention to the relationships of Christianity and Marxist scientific socialism in the revolutionary restructuring of social orders. In comparative fashion he asks what Marxism and Christianity offer. The essential difference is a Marxist model for confronting the growing disparity between the rich and the poor, a model Blanquart fails to discover in Christianity and its churches. His claim that it is not *a priori* necessary to identify

3

and hold in union atheism, socialism, and revolution, will certainly evoke controversy from both Christians and Marxists. Blanquart's favored alternative is a modified Marxism in which scientific socialism and atheism are not necessarily united or identified. His is the suggestion that Christians can be revolutionaries and even Marxists without being atheists.

Dutch sociologists P. L. Geschiere and H. G. Schulte Nordholt present a unique and comprehensive investigation of the phenomenology of revolution. Following a description of various developments in the sciences and social sciences for studying social phenomena (including the complex difficulties of defining revolution) they present eleven characteristics of revolutions, the situations in which revolutions may be generated, and the major types of revolutions. Phenomenological discussions of violence in revolutions and alternatives to violence are then explored. Concluding that the present methodologies for depicting revolutions remain quite flexible, they propose the model of a "revolutionary transformation of society." In developing this model Geschiere and Schulte Nordholt examine the potentials for political application of various tools including social-scientific grids and predictive graphs. It is not easy to overestimate the uses and potential values of this unique methodology for the future of world politics and revolutionary developments, because it proposes specific devices and methods for estimating, evaluating, describing, and predicting the course of revolutions.

Part III turns attention to recent experiences in revolution and in particular those of the Third World. A description of revolution in the Third World is given by Senegalese political writer Albert Paul Lentin. For him, the Third World can only be commonly identified geographically and as "that part of the world which is exploited" by the rest of the world. Following a brief but cogent historical review of revolutionary developments and the growth of socialist orders, Lentin asserts that socialism is the most feasible way of overcoming underdevelopment and that North American capitalism poses the most serious threat to the Third World's peoples and their future. This future is seen to exist in a strengthening of cooperative socialism that will challenge and overthrow existing economic patterns of world trade, production, and distribution. Lentin concludes with a forceful prognostication: a road of radical, armed contests in order to bring Third World peoples out of underdevelopment; a long escalation of violent activity including the growth of guerrilla wars; a worldwide clash of Third World peoples; then capitalism by the decade beginning in 1980.

The IDO-C dossier on revolution in Latin America follows Lentin's essay. Each document is introduced and set in context in the dossier, which is a broad collection of contemporary revolutionary materials taken from throughout Latin America.

The IDO-C Dossier on Violence and Revolution presents a representative selection of documents, largely from the Third World, that depict three major approaches to reform and restructuring of the social order: (1) evolutionary transformation that opposes violence; (2) nonviolent revolutions; (3) violent revolutions. The 1968 Pastoral Letter of the Chilean Bishops and a Pastoral Letter of Bishop Aguirre of Argentina forcefully contend that Christianity is opposed to violence; that justice must be sought through gradual transformations of the social order; and that respect for civil authority must govern all reforming activity.

Essays by Helder Camara, Cardinal Duval of Algiers, Jean Lasserre, and Miss Barbara Deming share a common affinity for the ideology and methodology of nonviolence. Violence is depicted as a menace to life and even where employed its methodology is regarded as a *via negativa*. The seeking of justice and truth through nonviolence is held to be a feasible and effective instrument for radical change of the social order.

The third and final group of documents represents the range of arguments and rationale for violent revolutions. Thomas Melville and Robert Cousso bluntly speak of nonviolence as a fading and ineffective method for change in the struggles for justice and human welfare. North American philosopher Herbert Marcuse speaks of forms of oppression that no class of the oppressed can tolerate; hence the genesis and justification for violent revolt and its ethos. Bertrand Duclos suggests a religious and nearly mystical motif in envisioning the violence of the poor

5

as sacrificial. Brazilian sociologist Jalles Costa finds violence as the only remaining alternative in the present world; nonviolent action becomes an accomplice of oppression. Finally, the dossier concludes with the direct call to violent action of the late Camilo Torres in his last letter to the Colombian peoples.

Pilgrim Press

Part I Can a Christian Be
        a Revolutionary?

Chapter One

The Gospels and
the Church as a
Revolutionary Force

Heinz Dietrich Wendland

The great revolutions of modern times, from the English to the Chinese, and not forgetting either the French or the Russian Revolution, have given a completely different face to the world in which we live. They have given birth to the modern society of liberty, equality, democracy, the society governed by the economy and by technology. The oriental revolutions have given rise to the organisms of the Communist society and the system of the totalitarian state. The effects of these revolutions lead up to the present era of political, social, and economic transformations in Asia, in Africa, and in Latin America; this is a revolution that is still in full course and its dimension and intensity are such as to give it a total and global character. We are not yet in a position to see the end of this general revolution that involves and shakes the whole world. We are all living in a transitional society and the exact picture of the society of tomorrow can as yet be glimpsed only in a few and rather vague general features.

ANTI-REVOLUTIONARIES IN THE NAME OF GOD

It would be logical to think that these historical upheavals, with their impact extending over more than three centuries, have aroused profound emotion in Christian thought; one would think that this thought had made efforts to seek the cause and the effects of these great revolutions. But, and this is a surprising fact, nothing of this kind has happened. It is true that there have been numerous discussions between the churches and some revolutionary movements, particularly after the French Revolution;

but for the greater part these debates have had a negative character. This situation changed after 1848, although only partially, when some theologians, pastors, and liberal members of the Church participated in activities aimed at obtaining democratic reforms in Germany. We should also point out that ever since the sixteenth century there have been theological theses regarding the right to resist a tyrannical authority—in certain cases these go as far as asserting the right to kill the tyrant—but these theological positions had nothing at all in common with the vast fact of revolution itself; in practice these positions only considered an abuse of power and the possibility that a once legitimate authority might so far forget its duties as to make opposition to it morally justified for a Christian.

The eminently negative character of Christian discussion about revolution is based on a strong tradition of conservative Christian thought that assumed a strong reactionary and restorative aspect during the nineteenth and twentieth centuries. It considers the traditional political and social order, and particularly the tasks of the princes and kings, to be sacrosanct and untouchable because they have been established and ordained by God. The words of the Apostle Paul with respect to the political powers of the authorities of the Roman Empire of his times are interpreted in a conservative sense as relating to a divine institution (*diatagé*).

Even the privileged castes of the clergy and the nobility are considered as consisting of people whom God himself has elevated to their position; the hierarchical structure of society is sanctified, sacralized, and everybody must remain in the social status that God has assigned to him, be it high or low on the social ladder. Every dynamism, every mobility, every form of social ascent are excluded with the sole exception of a few rare cases. Taking this point of view as a starting point, it is quite natural that revolution can only be judged as something to be condemned, even something that is criminal and directed not only against men, but against God and the universal order he has established once and for all.

The rejection of revolution on the part of conservative

Christianity is therefore a religious judgment, rather than a mere moral or political judgment. A more precise notion of revolution will permit us to subject this typical Christian conservatism to a well founded critique.

The Reality of Total Revolution

There is an enormous mass of definitions and attempts at describing the revolutionary phenomenon; for us it will be sufficient to mention a few of them that will enable us to evaluate some of the traditional and present positions of Christians.

One of the fundamental concepts is that of political revolution in the narrow sense; in this case we are simply dealing with the replacement of the people in power by other persons who take their place. This change of power comes about without arousing the idea that the political and social system should be changed; in fact, this system is not challenged ideologically, nor is it attacked in practice. The political revolution in this narrow sense therefore occurs within a general framework that is accepted without modification. But there is also the concept of the social revolution; some groups of the population who had been oppressed up to that moment, who had neither liberty nor a share in power, now take possession of power by using violence in a more or less manifest manner. They exclude the upper classes from the positions they held up to that moment and take their place. Social revolutions of this kind, quite obviously, also bring with them an upheaval of the political order.

The great social and political upheavals in medieval times belong to this phenomenon, as do the struggles between the patricians and the plebs, the passage from the monarchy to the republic, and many other upheavals that nevertheless remained rather limited. But what is really interesting is to see the appearance of the first ideological attacks against the upper class in the process of effectively bringing it down. The oppressed, the exploited, claim their freedom and equality of rights; they want a place of their own within the social context, they want their share of power in all sectors of life just like those who previously held the reins of society and led an easy life on the backs of the weak and the poor who had to work for them. The peasants in revolt in the course of the Peasant Wars at the time of the Reformation justified their social claims by basing themselves on the Gospels, asserting that the liberty and the equality of the sons of God must also determine the social order, which must therefore be modeled on the human community of Paradise. An old popular adage asked: "When Adam toiled and Eve spun, who was then the gentleman?"

The same motifs reappeared a century later, strengthened by the spiritualists and the members of the English revolutionary sects who were later to become the spiritual fathers of the American Revolution. It is therefore quite clear that Christianity not only has a conservative attitude with regard to revolution, but also a progressive and even revolutionary attitude.

In the eyes of these Christians the community founded by God's covenant with man is the People of God and its free and equal members represent the type on which the social and political order of the world must be founded, and this in opposition to the traditional society, hierarchically based on privilege. Political democracy must come into being from the spiritual "democracy" of the Kingdom of God on earth in the form of the Christian Church already at work among mankind, and it must continually renew itself. A Christian revolutionary thought thus comes into being through faith in the presence and the imminence of the Kingdom of God in the world through the Church; the effects of this thought have modeled modern English and American society, although they have done this through a whole series of secularizing processes.

The two types and attitudes of Christian thought, the conservative and the revolutionary, are now face to face in the present-day ecumenical movement. Neither has so far gained the upper hand; this will depend greatly on the theological positions they adopt and which will make it possible for individual Christians to make a practical choice.

There is a third type of revolution, which we shall call total revolution; in this case we are dealing with the transformation of the entire social system. This transformation affects all the elements of society and all sectors of life including culture, spiritual life, and religion.

This is a revolution brought about by the force of the technical and scientific civilization of our times and it now tends to assume worldwide dimensions; it is a total revolution not only by virtue of its extent, but also on account of its intensity and its force of penetration. In fact, it is based on a new relationship between man and the world, and within this relationship man appears as essentially revolutionary because it is within his power to radically change the history of the world; he is practically the creator of a second artificial universe.[1] The technical and scientific civilization begins by changing the relationship between man and nature, then it changes the relationship between man and man, the relationship of man to his work, and lastly it changes man himself through technology, science, applied psychology and the use of new psychological and sociological concepts.

Man ends up by changing himself into a conditioned being of which both present and future society stand in need in accordance with the system that has been created. This means that the creator and transformer of the new world, harnessed to technology, formed and known through rational science, becomes slave of himself, and deprives himself of liberty to the extent to which he wants to live in the conditions imposed by the system he himself has created: the machines, the techniques, the scientific methods, the social organizations. The creator is this creator of himself, and must obey the laws he has made for creating his world. In this way there appears the creative power, but there appears also the menace that weighs upon man in our technical world of scientific civilization. Man thus unchains the "creative power of destruction" for which no limit can seemingly be established.[2]

It is precisely this notion of total revolution that emerges from all the other notions of revolution by means of which one may describe the facts and the types of modification to which societies and states are subject.

We are thus led to admit that revolution is not an evolution, i.e., it is not a gradual and organic development that proceeds by stages. In fact, revolution can also be a passage to evolution, as is shown by the English and American Revolutions. But we must nevertheless distinguish clearly between these two notions. Evolution presupposes a social system that it does not overturn, but which it develops gradually in the course of a certain period of time and according to the energies it has at its disposal. We must also distinguish revolution from reform or from a global situation understood as a long-term general plan of reform. Reform, too, presupposes a social system that has already become historical fact; it faces up to improvements that affect the various institutions; these improvements are based on critical considerations regarding society put forward by the various political and social movements within that society itself. This critique of the existing institutions and social conditions may well have its roots in the critical thought of the social ethics of Christians and the churches; or, rather, we think that this should be the case and that one should make efforts to achieve collaboration between Christian social critique and profane social critique. Reaction is to be found at the opposite pole; it attempts to repress revolution and its effects, presenting it ideologically through an anti-critique as something unjust, illegitimate and, above all, as morally reprehensible. Hannah Arendt has rightly shown that it owes its existence to the French Revolution.[3] In fact, reaction is by its nature polemical, and we might also add that it is negative, sterile, and quite incapable of creating new forms; moreover, reaction's baggage of notions is of a "derived nature."[4]

We must, however, distinguish between conservatism and reaction, in spite of the fact that they are historically related. Conservatism, too, is entirely dependent on the revolutionary phenomenon, it seeks to maintain or to restore the social order that existed prior to the revolution. It lives by a prescientific myth of nature that can also be colored by a Christian conception (the state of creation); National Socialism (the Nazis) made use of this myth in its secularized form: the community of the people, the unity of the Führer, the people, the blood, and the fatherland.

European anti-revolutionary and conservative romanticism has often given this myth a form that is rich in thought and has lent it some historical elements; it allied itself in a particular way with Protestant theology during the nineteenth century and rigorously laid down its political and social behavior. Paul Tillich subjected this conservative "original myth" to a fundamental critique that is still valid today;[5] the same theologian had already pointed out during the nineteen-twenties the relationship that existed between Christian nationalism and this original myth.

To the extent to which conservative thought starts from the preservation of the past, the traditional identifies with everything that is proved and true (it "gathers ancient truth," says Goethe), it is widely founded in a polemical sense; all the same, it does not derive its strength only from antithesis, as is the case of reaction, but rather from historical traditions that it would be dangerous to despise and from a realistic appreciation of man. Conservatism has an irresistible tendency towards every kind of optimistic utopia. Anti-revolutionary romanticism is not the only one to have had a content of conservative thought; even such a perspicacious person as Søren Kierkegaard conceives revolution as the moral decadence of humanity, and Feodor Stepun, in the second volume of his memoirs *Vergängliches und Unvergängliches,* characterizes revolution as "a mixture of crime and illness" by means of the picture he draws of the February Revolution in Russia in 1917.

For this kind of thinking, revolution represents a collapse, a dissolution, a decadence, the decomposition of the organic community of the people and the state, the end of morality and religion, the end of every true culture and the despising of history; every value, everything that is noble and great is irremediably lost through revolution. These lamentations still resound in the pessimistic criticisms of culture during the first twenty years of the century.

15

There is only one thing that is correct in these criticisms: a large number of values does effectively disappear in all the great historical changes and is never restored or recovered; these values belong irrevocably to the past. But from the Christian point of view these disappearances, these losses, are part of the very nature of history, which is the history of men, of institutions and of empires, and all these are mortal.

Revolutionary consciousness evidently expresses itself in a diametrically opposed manner. In this case man is the creator of his future and that of mankind, and frees himself from traditional historical weights and from the chaos of laws and regulations that have accumulated in the course of a long history. It is man who opens the door to the future, who constructs a better society (even though it may not be perfect), who creates a just state in which liberty, equality, justice, and humanity hold the central place.

The explanation that revolution gives of itself is linked with the socio-political utopia of the eventually perfect state and the idea of the natural revolutionary and radical right; in the first place it talks of the new future that revolution opens for humanity; in the second place it speaks of the origin of revolution in the rational and creative nature of man, here understood as the criterion by which every historical order must be measured because it is precisely through this nature that any given order loses its absolute value and its dominion over man.

Human reason elaborates and creates law, the state and society in their definitive and true form. At the end of the revolutionary process one arrives at the reign of liberty of man who has fully matured in all his faculties, the reign of rational culture and of justice that makes the revolutionary act accessible and present. This, in broad outline, is the secular and eschatological consciousness that revolution has of itself. This is clearly visible in the case where it is considered as absolute revolution, for example in Marx.

The victory of the proletariat puts an end to the prehistory of mankind, opens the door to the reign of liberty and at the same time leads to the unfailing satisfaction of all human needs.

Here begins the history of man in the true sense of the word, because the contradiction between the nature and the existence of man is at last brought to an end, contradiction that for long ages was the cause of his suffering. To this dominion of liberty without any restriction corresponds absolute man, creator, freed from every suffocation, creator of an authentically human world that eliminates all the alienations of man vis-à-vis himself, his fellows, his work and the products of his work, and also frees him from the chains of nature.[6]

THE CHOICE BETWEEN GOD AND THE DEVIL

Karl Marx has developed the notion of absolute revolution; moreover, he has forged the concept of revolution that has most extensively and incisively made history and has brought into being the organs of Communist society. Revolution eliminates the old history of class struggles and creates a homogeneous, classless society. The triumphant dictatorship of the proletariat is the historical midwife that brings this society into being. The destructive dualism of the two classes, capitalism and the proletariat, ceases to exist. We have already mentioned the reign of liberty or of the self-creation of man, which frees him from every alienation, servitude and submission; the absolute revolution also represents man's elevation to the absolute, and it is he who constructs himself and shapes society. This man is the messiah of himself in the form of the collectivity, i.e., the proletariat.

This conception, according to which the proletariat revolution was the sense and the end of all history, has unleashed a missionary force of hitherto unknown vigor and still operates in all the fields of misery and in all the systems of feudal oppression as a force of fermentation, upheaval and transformation, particularly in Asia, in Africa and Latin America. This means that we find ourselves in the midst of a process of total world revolution that is extending to all the continents and is overturning all the old civilizations and the ancient systems of society with an irresistible force through the means of technology and rational science. There is no longer any remedy against this revolutionary dynamic; at the best there are only some means of slowing it

17

down. Inasmuch as we are here dealing with the dynamics of technology and science, things are at the same point both in the East and the West, and this in spite of all the differences of political and social structure.

At the opposite end of the scale we find the conception of revolution originated by Friedrich Julius Stahl (1802–61), the inspirer of Prussian conservatism, a conception that he explains in his *Philosphie des Rechts*. Stahl completely follows the formula of Gottfried Menken, the preacher of the "awakening" from Bremen: "All revolutions are aimed against the Kingdom of God." From Menken and Stahl onwards this has been the leitmotif of all Christian conservative thought, and Stahl was the first to provide it with a theological and juridical foundation. It is a conception that founds its doctrine of law and the state on the "Christian conception of the world," a conception that Stahl bases on the authority of God, here understood as a "personality." Revolution is therefore against God and against the order he has established; it is the work of man who rebels against God; it is man who wants to put his own sovereignty in place of God's. Therefore revolution is the demonstration of human sin.

And yet this conception does not prevent Stahl from seeing clearly and correctly in certain particular situations; he definitely recognized the absolute and permanent character of the contemporary revolution. On the other hand, one cannot reproach him with only having considered revolution as something negative; on the contrary, he made efforts to render justice to the well-founded claims of his times for a relative liberty of the subjects of the constitution; he remains the passionate defender of sovereign legitimacy, particularly in Prussia, but in contrast with absolutism seeks to construct a right to liberty for the members of the state, even though his assertions may appear rather timid to us. We can see in them a modernization of the old territorial freedoms, rather than true democratic thought.

This conception of Stahl exercised a profound influence on his times, on German conservatism of the twenties and on Protestant theology right up to the publication of Walter Künneth's book *Politik zwischen Dämon und Gott* in 1954. The anti-revolutionary spirit has become so virulent as to make it almost impossible even in our own times to have an unprejudiced discussion between Christian thought on the one hand, and the phenomenon of revolution and the ideas that sustain it on the other. The worst consequence has been that of closing the great churches within themselves, and making them quite impermeable to both democracy and socialism.

Christian thinking and its social ethics could well have brought great and fecund possibilities for the transformation and development of the ideas of the revolutionary movements; but theology and the Church installed themselves in the field of the dominant powers of monarchy and, in the social and political field they preferred to place themselves by the side of the bourgeoisie and the large corporations.

But the total character of the world revolution forces us into the discussion that had been continually postponed up to now; it can no longer be avoided, on the contrary, it is being continually called for, and rightly so, by Christians in Asia and Africa who are being subjected to the consequences of the social transformation in their countries, in their populations, in their churches, and even in their bodies. In this way a large number of wholly new problems are posing themselves for the social ethics of the immediate future.[7]

The victory that Stahl's conception won in the political and social thinking of German Christianity cannot therefore be a final one. We are forced to ask ourselves whether we accept and recognize as positive certain elements of truth to be found in the revolutionary conception of Karl Marx.

The national socialist (Nazi) revolution is ideologically determined; it corresponds to the Marxist notion of revolution, although it is very far from it. Nevertheless, it is total, invades every field of life, and consequently must inevitably come into conflict with the Church. In the course of this struggle the Church was forced to realize that this was not by any means a case of freedom to preach the Gospels or to assemble for the purpose of religious service, but rather a question of the state of society itself, of its liberties and its just institutions. In Germany one quickly became aware of the gaps in Protestant theology, which had not elaborated a system of social ethics capable of facing up to modern problems and circumstances and consequently found itself desperately short of points of support when it came to grips with the problems of revolution. It thus misunderstood national socialism at the beginning, and considered it as a conservative movement of national renewal that sought to establish an authoritative (and authoritarian) state in place of the anarchy of the political parties. The traditional concept of authority made the churches quite incapable of understanding the revolutionary aspect of national socialism. This conservatism and authoritarian thought even have a strong influence on the ecclesiastic resistance movement of the *Bekennende Kirche* (the "confessing church"); it did not follow a really democratic idea, but rather that of a purified totalitarian state of justice and liberty. A Christian conception of revolution did not develop in the "Confessing Church," although this would have constituted a good reply to national socialism and would have been a useful contribution to criticizing its ideology and its actions.

In the meantime it was continually becoming more obvious that the problems of modern society could not be faced by starting from the position of the doctrine of the two kingdoms. We know today that one cannot abandon the economy, society and civilization to the discretion of the state, but that we must make the Church responsible for humanizing them and ensuring that they will behave in the interest of society as a whole.

CHRISTIANITY FACED BY THE TENDENCIES TOWARD TOTAL REVOLUTION

We have already noted the total character of the revolutionary process of our times. This is the revolution provoked by the technical and scientific civilization, by rationalism and by gradual industrialization. It is a revolution that reaches all continents, transforms all the traditions and institutions, and penetrates the most ancient civilizations. It forces all the world's religions to undergo a hard test of truth such as they have never faced before, and to transform their morality and their social ethics in conformity with the new human and social facts. The struggle between the mythological language in which the religions express themselves and the spirit of rational philosophy has entered into a new and possibly decisive phase.

As regards Asia and Africa, the Church and its missions constitute an important element that has contributed towards this revolution. In fact, through its teaching and training institutions, the Church has introduced European and American civilization to these continents and has thus contributed towards forming a new intellectual elite. Once again Christianity has revealed itself as an element of revolutionary ferment in the cultures and social systems with which it has come into contact. This process was only momentarily brought to a halt and stabilized, for example in the form of the "tribal churches" in Africa; according to the principle of union between the Church and the state these churches would correspond to the national churches in Europe, but they are now about to dissolve and must leave their place to new forms of ecclesial communities. Even though it may not be possible for the moment to list all the elements in this "global" revolution, we may at least mention the more important.

Above all, the crisis has been provoked by the partial dissolution of the "great family" by virtue of the Western principle of individualism, free choice of one's marriage partner and the conclusion of a (formal) marriage, which causes a displacement and a metamorphosis of the juridical and social forms of marriage. The small family of modern times, structured on the association of two partners, is beginning to gain the day, particularly in the great African cities; woman's position is gradually becoming freer and more independent, she is gradually freeing herself from man's domination and therefore can no longer be either a piece of property or an object of commerce.

In addition to this we have the revolution of the agricultural economy brought about by the introduction of machines and scientific and technical methods into agriculture. This implies a new and above all rational relationship between man and the land; the transformation of the economy results in new social structures and these radically modify the community life of the village and the tribal customs.

Next, we see the constitution of numerous new states that seek to exploit Western ideas and political constitutions; for this reason they are continually torn between dictatorship and democracy. It is quite clear that when the conditions of civilization and of training for democracy are still lacking, beginning with even the most elementary ones (reading, writing, etc.), the adaptation of the constitutional forms of democracy must be artificial and democracy cannot therefore function. The ideological influences that have come from the West are extremely strong; this is particularly noticeable in the flames of nationalism in Asia and Africa. Although the European idea of nations and national liberty is based on quite different historical and social conditions, nationalism has acted in an overwhelming manner in numerous transformations and still constitutes the most important ferment of the new state structures. Without the great integrating force of the idea of a nation it would not be possible to overcome the tribal limits and the great social and cultural differences that exist within these new states; the numerous Christians that are involved in political action in these continents provide striking confirmation of this.

Nevertheless, the central problem is that of the overall order of the new society and the place that man occupies in it. The need for giving the initiative and the direction of the operations for the constitution of new economic organisms to the state implies the appearance of the most varied forms of national socialism and of attempts to establish a more or less socialistic economic and social order. Whether anything durable and of practical application will come out of all this is still rather uncertain.

In connection with this last point, there frequently appears an age-old and religious idea of collective salvation, a kind of "social" redemption, in which Christian, Marxist, and old pagan elements are fused into a singular whole. Prophets, healers, and sects proliferate among an unpredictable mass, and this renders all description impossible; many of these have a rather short existence or reach only a very small circle of partisans and adorers.

The ancient world religions, Christianity, Islam, Hinduism, and Buddhism, find themselves forced by this situation to reexamine their morality and their social ethics, and to modify them for the first time (this is the case with Buddhism). Moreover, the non-Christian world religions are absorbing numerous elements of Christianity, because it seems to them that such ideas as permeated with Western Christianity as liberty, humanity, justice, social and political peace, a society worthy of man, and political and social equality, are all absolutely essential in the building up of new states and new social units. It is therefore necessary to unite them as closely as possible with the ancient and autochthonous traditions in the religious and moral fields and thus to insert the authority of the old traditions into the new way of thinking and acting, if possible without a break.

All these phenomena clearly show the total character of this revolution which shakes and transforms the whole world; not even the religions can escape. New forms of the state, of society and of culture are brought into being by it; its strongest tendency is that of creating one civilization and a worldwide uniform society.

The Christians and the churches of the developing countries (and also of other countries) face up to this revolutionary process in different ways, but they do it while being obviously ill at ease, with incomprehension and indecision. In this connection, Karl Heinz Pfeffer's *Welt im Umbruch* (Gütersloh, 1966) is full of information and teachings. This anxious and hesitant attitude is the natural result of the lack of a modern system of social ethics and a Christian conception of revolution either in a positive or a critical sense. The traditional principles of ecclesiastic thought, such as those concerning the authoritarian state, democracy, economic liberalism, the conservative ideology of the "community," etc., block the road towards social ethics that conform to the real situation and delay the comprehension of the present world revolution.

In the face of this sterile and very negative attitude that

23

makes every coordinated action quite impossible, the churches will have to bear certain needs well in mind. They will have to elaborate a global and critical conception of the world revolution that is now taking place and which, with all its various tendencies and different forces, is receiving its inspiration from Christian ethics together with all the other interested sciences.

In this connection it is also particularly necessary and urgent to formulate a theological theory of revolution; for our own part, we are trying to make a contribution by suggesting a few lines in this essay. A penetrating critique of all the liberal, socialist, conservative and reactionary theories and of all the ideologies of society and revolution will undoubtedly contribute towards the preparation of the twofold task we have just mentioned.

Quite apart from theological theory and social ethics, the churches must be inspired by an action of solidarity with the world so that they will come to be concerned with serving oppressed men, with problems of the new order and the general order of society, problems that are raised wherever the revolutionary process is in course; this is in the first place a case of having the courage of one's faith, the courage of looking freely and openly towards the future and the tasks that it imposes.

If the churches are to have this attitude it will be necessary to make clear the plan of action and its future-oriented character in such a way that its purpose may be understood by a society that is conscious of its responsibilities and measures and judges all situations and orders according to the moral and social criteria of liberty, justice, human partnership and peace.

What has been said above is also valid for Christians in rapidly developing countries; side by side with a small minority that stands out on account of its openness and its participation in social and political action, there is the great majority of those who are without a point of support, without liberty and without guarantees, and who stand in need of a radical transformation of the sense of life if they want to comply today with the command of loving their neighbors.

The Kingdom of God Against the Present Form of the World

The essential question that arises today from the theological point of view is that of the revolutionary element contained in the Gospels themselves and of the effect that it has on human history. If this has taken on a revolutionary character in recent times, we are immediately faced with another question regarding the relationship between the revolutionary content of the Gospels and the revolution in a historical sense. Is there contradiction and hostility between them, do they evolve in two totally opposed dimensions, one spiritual and the other earthly? Or is it possible to link them in some way or other? We would like to offer a few points of view that might contribute towards the answer.

Paul Tillich is the first and possibly the only theologian of note who has seen the problem and has dedicated his attention to it.[8] He finds his starting point in the eschatological hope of primitive Christianity: this awaits the Kingdom to come, the domination of God over the entire world; this Kingdom has become historical and present in Jesus Christ and in the form of his community, i.e., the Church. Even now it already modifies and transforms this world of man and its history through the new creation, the creation of the end of time.

The Kingdom does not only concern the individual or the inner life, the morality and the religion of man, but rather conceives the human universe as a spatial and temporal *totum* from which nothing is excluded. There is nothing either material or external that does not stand in relationship with this Kingdom; the universality of the sovereignty of God involves the whole of his creation and tends to liberate it from sin and death and to bring it towards fulfillment.

The Kingdom of God is therefore in contrast with the present form of this world to the extent to which this latter does not correspond to the holy and life-giving will of God and is characterized by sin and death. The sense of this opposition to the world is not the creation of a political constitution that has not yet been written or of a perfect social order that would eliminate all the evil caused by poverty, injustice and oppression, but rather the universal fulfillment of the justice and the love of God, which become one and the same thing in God and his sovereignty. This will of God is directed to the person and the heart of man in the Son and Heir of God and of his Kingdom. But man in his totality, body and soul, and with his historical, social and political existence is involved in this event, so that the duality of the body and the spirit, of the interior and the exterior, of man and world, becomes cancelled. The ethical and social effects are therefore imminent in the coming of this Kingdom and emanate from this coming.

These effects are as if they were placed in the keeping of the historical community of Christ, which is in the world not only as a community of faith and hope, but also as a community of service in the love of Christ and which acts in the conviction that all men are neighbors. It understands its mission towards the world not only as a mission (however important this fundamental aspect may be), but at the same time also as a task of solicitude for man, and particularly for man suffering from poverty and privation.

As a manifestation of the grace and the glory of God, the Kingdom is always more than a simple moral act or a communion brought into being by such an act; it transcends and goes beyond all criteria, all ideas and all social notions of a moral quality. And yet, the force and the ethical and social effectiveness are imminent in it. According to its own nature it engages in the struggle against every form of injustice and poverty, and against every form of oppression of man; it fights for the construction of man in his truth and in his humanity and against all the innumerable historical deformations to which man has been subject.

The sovereignty of God, as understood in this sense, has an "indirect" action that is socially and politically revolutionary, not by arousing rebellion or using political or military power, but solely through an action that is free from violence, an action of love and of service of the Christian communities that are dispersed in the world, but constitute a unity in Christ. These assertions are therefore opposed to the Christian utopianism that believes in the creation of the Kingdom of Christ in this world through the action of Christians. However, it is not the Church that builds Christ's Kingdom of life and grace, although Christ himself serves all Christians, his disciples, and sustains their action with the strength of the Holy Spirit. In this world and its history the Kingdom of Christ remains in struggle against sin, against the flesh and against death, and it will therefore remain forever incomplete. Only the end of history, brought about by God in Christ, will bring the fulfillment of the Kingdom to the world. But its presence, the pressure that it exerts and the shock it causes in history, channels the world towards its ends, puts it into continual movement and maintains it in living expectation. The active transformation of the world, although eschatologically limited, is already operating in humanity, even though its full extent is as yet hidden. It therefore represents an eschatological behavior that opposes basic needs and the force of love to all the realities of the world or transforms them in a creative manner, according to times and circumstances.

This behavior, through its prophecy of the end and its radical claims, destroys every *myth of origin* that appeals to the forces of origin, birthplace, life, blood or race. It even annihilates the isolated faith in creation that identifies such a world with the creation of God and abandons itself to the illusion that it can allow the pure life forces of Paradise to run. Only Christ can open the doors of Paradise and give eternal life.

Thus the Kingdom of God is the incomplete Kingdom that struggles in history by means of love and the Spirit; it suffers numberless defeats on account of man's incredulity and sin, on account of the insufficient faith and courage of the Christians, but it is and remains invincible because it lives in the world of the presence of Christ and no worldly force can weaken it. We thus have the fundamental Christian paradox of death and resurrection, of victory without victory, of triumph in seeming defeat, which also determines the character of eschatological ethics. The countless prophets that have foretold the end of Christianity have shown themselves to be false prophets; they would remain such even if millions of men should believe in the predictions.

Arthur Rich also follows in a certain sense the fundamental thought of the eschatological *ethos* that transforms the world. On the one hand he opposes the conception of the absolute revolution and the absolutization of man. On the other hand he understands the fact of being a Christian as a revolutionary existence in love and in justice, and in the preservation of humanity for the good of man. The preservation of the status quo, absenteeism, complicity with existing conditions, are all things that betray the critical and revolutionary element of Christian existence. "The Christian faith, by virtue of its eschatological nature, liberates a revolutionary humanity."[9] This revolutionary Christian existence does not aim at a "social order of a final character." The love that characterizes the Christian faith is not anti-revolutionary; it tends towards a concrete improvement of everything that is relative and historical; it therefore transposes the love (*agape*) of Christ into humanity. In this manner Arthur Rich arrives at a revolutionary Christian humanism that is neither utopian nor absolute. Consciously and rightly he goes beyond the limits of current theological ethics that have given insufficient consideration to the problem of revolution on account of their failure to start from the concept of the future sovereignty of God and of his justice as the fundamental engagement of man.[10]

THE SOCIAL AND THEOLOGICAL ENGAGEMENT OF REVOLUTIONARY CHRISTIAN HUMANISM

It seems essential to us that the line of thought begun by Tillich and Rich should be elaborated and followed further; we think that this can be done through a reflection about revolutionary Christian humanism and its social and theological engagement.

First of all, this engagement must be understood in an eschatological sense; this means that the Kingdom of God comes into the world with the commandment of justice and the gift of unselfish love, the form of which is essentially that of service. On account of its love for man and his real historical future, the community of Christ engages its action in favor of liberty, justice and humanity, even though these realities may only succeed in assuming a relative and institutional form. But a single drop of humanity and justice has an immensely greater value than the merciless passivity of inhumanity and injustice. All human institutions can be modified, none of them has a fixed or untouchable value. In the intervention of the Church that requires the institutions of society to be improved according to the criteria of justice and love there is a preparatory action of the just sovereignty of God that is showing itself. This function must be carried out by the "Christianity" of the whole world; it is the duty of all Christians who work in society, in the state, in the economy or in culture to do this through their offices and their occupations. Each of them carries within him a function (i.e., his occupation) that God has entrusted to him in the service of a society in continual reform, i.e., with a view to reforming and improving the institutions of society. Christians must not ask themselves whether the success of their actions is great or small, whether they will have a long-lasting or merely transitory effect; they must carry out the mission of serving man and society that God has entrusted them, and they must do this whatever may be the mission or the historical situation. They try to eliminate poverty and suffering, particularly the more hidden forms of suffering; they are the "deacons" of the world, they must be the pioneers of every social reform.

This theological and social engagement in favor of a revolutionary Christian humanism must be considered as an anthropological engagement. God has put man into the world as *co-operator Dei*, God's cooperator, enriching him with the capacity of giving a form to the world. Man's infinite power vis-à-vis the world derives from this force; he is the administrator, organizer and reformer of the state, the economy and society. He is prepared for this task by his reason, which recognizes the world, analyzes it and structures it by means of a critical judgment, even though this reason, as Luther observes, is incapable of saving man from sin and death. But in the world this reason is competent, it has the power and the right to act. This anthropological conception of our engagement in the field of social ethics must then be completed and limited: the Christian and the Church, by virtue of their pneumatic and eschatological existence, have the mission of loving the world and serving it. This mission is connected with the creative function of *cooperator Dei,* although its origin is different and derives from the Kingdom of Christ. The particular fecundity and the extraordinary force of Christian action in history is the result of this union of the two ministries.

The ethical and social engagement must also be considered and judged from the point of view of the rules of action (the *ethos*). In this sense we have to describe the duty of Christians, and more particularly that of the Christian community of service, as contributing with their actions to the reform of social institutions. Christians are not alone, but they are co-responsible; the state and society are not the creations of Christianity, they are autonomous and are guided by a law that is peculiar to them; but Christians, together with the others, must shoulder the responsibility for the forms and the social and political institutions.

One should also add that Christians are placed into a relationship with the already existing forms in the world in which they live that is both positive and critical. They are jointly responsible with all men who exercise the same political, social or economic functions that they themselves exercise. But this solidarity remains critical in the sense that it comports an effective protest against every injustice and every inhumanity. The critical solidarity therefore expresses itself in Christians being available for every possibility of reform that might delineate itself in the future. This availability in favor of the historical future of society forms a part of the very nature of the collaboration of Christians in society. It is sustained by the certainty that God has left the history of mankind with a door open towards the future and that numerous and as yet unknown possibilities will present themselves as regards the order and formation of society.

In this way Christians are also free to study both detailed plans and overall plans, because the splitting up of their actions into partial reforms could well deprive Christian action of its force and incisiveness. The overall plans will determine both the sense and the particular point of insertion of more detailed measures.

But the most important question is that of the purpose and the criteria of the overall Christian action in the service of the state and of society. We here want to talk of a historical plan, i.e., a plan that can be put into practice rather than an unreal utopia, a general guide that has a real point of insertion in historical reality and the positive possibilities that are to be found in it, just as it can be inserted in the negative aspects, in the critical situations of this reality. The ecumenical movement has made an effort to define this general directive and has followed the lines suggested by the formula of the "responsible society" ever since the World Council of Churches Assemblies at Amsterdam (1948) and Evanston (1954).[11]

This objective designates a democratically constituted society, based on human dignity, that judges itself according to the norms of liberty, justice, the human community and peace, and also accepts to obey these norms. The foundation stone of such a society is the free person, responsible before God and before men, who is called upon to offer a free and responsible collaboration in the state and in society and is also capable of assuming such a responsibility.

An elite of men and of nations must lay the foundations of the "responsible society" and although such a society may still be a thing of the future, it is already concretely engaged in the present. This elite will have to establish the conditions of the democratic state and the democratic society where they as yet exist only in embryo, for example in Asia, in Africa, and in Latin America.

In the process of translating a revolutionary Christian humanism of this kind into practice it will be possible to highlight and give additional value to the heredity of Christian communities of a revolutionary character, such as that of the English Revolution and of Puritanism. These communities were capable of see-

31

ing God's redeeming alliance with man in the form of the community of Christ as the prototype and the foundation of the alliance that unites all men in society.

The liberty of the sons of God, eschatologically and pneumatically founded in the Church, must make it possible for liberty and political and social equality to express themselves in the members of the state and society. Free Christians must and want to be free citizens. This relationship determines the political and social action of the Church, which aims at a democratic society that gives freedom and equality to all men.

A Critical and Positive Attitude Toward the Dynamic Revolutionary Society

In this action it is nevertheless essential to have a critical conscience. In fact, Christian action must not identify the Kingdom of God with society; the freedom of the world, the particular form of the state and of society must be safeguarded. For the same reason Christians must not make a "Christian revolution" but must always work with earthly and human instruments, such as politics and the law, for the necessary and ceaseless reform and for the transformation of society to the benefit of man. They therefore remain within the limits imposed upon them by this world; they do not build up "Christian" states, orders or societies; their task is the humanization of the earthly order,[12] and the real but rather modest progress that can be made in this field is more important than the more perfect Christian utopia, because such progress represents a concrete help given to real men and to real groups in society.

The Christianization of the regimes of this world will never be anything other than a mistaken diversion from the real task and an untruthful transfiguration. The Christian can only be applied to the activities of Christians who continually inject love into the humanity of the world. A critical and positive relationship, characterized by a sense of responsibility towards the dynamic and revolutionary society of present times, becomes possible only if Christians are capable of accepting both in theory and practice all the possibilities of the gradual transformation of society.

At this point, however, there is undoubtedly need for some critical reflection. Christians in their actions must not allow themselves to be guided by the ideology of the absolute revolution, and even less so by the utopia of the perfect society. This also means that they will not be able to effect an upheaval of all relationships by means of the use of force or violence, but rather that they totally accept the road of true reforms. But if Christians exclude recourse to the use of violence from their action for transforming the world, and more particularly the use of arms, this does not mean that they believe in the possibility of a society deprived of force or a state devoid of the means for governing; they certainly do not abandon themselves to this utopia. The order and the character of humanity cannot be preserved in a society without the creation of power and its use. But this power must be maintained within certain norms and linked to the service of the global objective, i.e., the humanization of society, the improvement of law and peace on both the social and the international level.

The criteria of humanity, liberty and justice must govern the use of power and the behavior of those who exercise it. When this happens the use of force becomes superfluous, and the simultaneous and "prophylactic" change of society eliminates the social and political causes that could lead to the use of violence.

THE CHURCH AS A PERMANENT SOURCE OF REVOLUTIONARY CHANGES

A spontaneous doubt arises after the observation we have made above: does this not involve the abandonment of the revolutionary spirit on which we have previously so strongly insisted?

An answer to this doubt must in the first place put the accent on the maintenance of the relationship between the particular reforms, which must be carried out one by one, and the general plan to which they are subordinated, the precise overall objective to be attained. In fact, only this latter guarantees the sense and the fecundity of the individual reforms, and enables those who have engaged themselves to preserve the vision of the global transformation that has to be achieved; in this way they do not dissipate their activities in excessively disjointed undertakings. It is true that the global plan cannot be achieved except through detailed interventions, but it is equally true that these interventions acquire their force and their truth only within the overall framework of a plan. The detailed measures and the partial reforms must be continually overhauled in the light of the ultimate purpose and the overall plan, and they must be adjusted according to this criterion. Only in this way can one avoid running the risk of seeing Christian humanism fall back on a simple reformism that proceeds on a hand to mouth basis by means of disjointed and detailed measures. It will remain revolutionary if it is inspired by the new overall order of society.

But, in contrast with the ideology of the absolute revolution, this new order is new only in a relative and historical sense; it is not extraneous to history and does not pretend to put an end to history. This global order is not in the sense of a new epoch in history, in the sense of new motives, of a new way of uniting the political forces and the social groups. The absolute novelty of the utopia that the absolute revolution pretends to achieve is nothing other than an illusory appearance; it cannot therefore merit the noble name of revolution. The true revolution is the one that bases itself on real history, does not escape from it, but rather introduces a new epoch and a new type of social order into this history.

For this reason it is essential to stress the clear distinction that exists between revolutionary Christian humanism and a reformism that consists of fragmentary corrections devoid of an overall objective; between this humanism and the absolute revolution and the absolute man it wants to create; between this humanism and the idea of a static conservatism and the pseudo-Christian equivalence; between the world and God's creation on which it bases itself; and lastly, between this humanism and totally negative reaction as the extreme opposite of absolute revolution.

In conformity with what has already been said, true revolutionary Christian humanism rather consists of certain elements that could be summarized as follows: its historicity, i.e., our relationship with its real engagement in historical society; its orientation towards an achievable objective, the plan of a relatively new and historical society; the carrying out of a positively responsible action of love and justice; the creation of this attitude out of the eschatological hope in the Kingdom of God that is to come and is present in history; the love that each day transforms itself into the human practice of help and reform.

At the beginning we stated the problem in these terms: the Church and revolution. Are we now in a position briefly to propose a solution, and if so, on which lines? The mission of the Church in the world and for the world leads it to a revolutionary, ethical and social action in the sense we have described, and in this way, as the Church of God in the world, it becomes the origin and the permanent source of revolutionary change in the state and in society. Because it was itself born out of the eschatological and revolutionary force of the Gospels, its attitude towards the historical revolution is such as to be at the same time both positive and critical. On the one hand it adopts and assumes the revolution, on the other hand it goes beyond it by discarding every utopian ideology. It does not dispose of the creation of God as is done by natural law, but it understands this creation in a realistic manner as a preexisting history, as a historical possibility, the basis of every concrete action.

Perhaps these are the essential elements that describe the social and theological engagement that would put the Church in a position not to oppose the total revolution of our times and by means of this opposition to constitute a brake on the overall revolutionary process; an engagement that would rather permit it to respond in a critical and positive manner to the needs of the revolution and even to go beyond it by means of a Christian revolutionary action in accordance with the guiding vision of the "responsible society."

The Decisive Theological Question in the Face of Revolution

We have said that the Church was born out of the eschatological and revolutionary force of the Gospels and that it therefore assumes a positive and critical attitude towards historical revolution. The decisive theological problem is therefore that of determining the nature of the social and theological engagement in the light of the Gospels, here understood as the message of the New Testament.

First of all, it should be obvious that the position we have adopted has nothing whatever to do with "Bible punching," because it refuses every form of legalistic abuse of the New Testament.

Moreover, it is clear that we do not intend to transform the eschatological message of the coming of the Kingdom of God in Jesus Christ and of his community, the Church, into a socio-moral utopia of a Christian society; rather we do want to keep intact the frontiers between the Kingdom of God and the world, between the opposition of the Kingdom to sin and the opposition of the world to death. In the same way we refuse the attitude of eschatological passivity, expectation without any transforming action on the world, because in this attitude of expectation we see a perversion of eschatological hope. Lastly, from the coming of the Kingdom of God into the world and the pneumatic character of the Church of Christ we deduce the right to use Christian freedom in the world, to use free Christian action in favor of the world, a freedom that manifests itself in love in the midst of historical and social structures and their transformation.

This means that we take account of the historical discontinuity of the times within the framework of the continuity of the Church. As Christians we must act within the world of contemporary technological and scientific civilization, within the dynamic and secular industrial society, and if necessary take account of the innumerable historical differences with respect to the society of the last few centuries, the society of antiquity or at the time of the Apostles. Any other attitude would mean that

Christians condemn themselves to servitude and prevent themselves from taking any action that is suited to man and the situation. And this would completely contradict their eschatological and pneumatic liberty; it would strangle and render useless any form of Christian ethics for the present times. Surely, this cannot be the meaning of the faith, of love and of hope.

We cannot give practical effect to our obedience with respect to achieving the salvation offered by God in Jesus Christ either by a simple repetition of the New Testament message, nor by a mere imitation of New Testament ethics. We must bear witness to the faith, to love and hope in the Holy Spirit, and we must do this today and in our modern society and with full trust in the presence of Christ in the world. From the liberty of the faith and the liberty of love derives our freedom to serve present-day man and to contribute towards the formation of our society.

Chapter Two Revolution and Violence

Almeri Bezerra de Melo

Only a short time after the most progressive Christian groups had made every kind of effort in order to ensure that the Vatican II Council would condemn war beyond any possibility of misunderstanding and without ambiguous words, thus burying once and for all the old theories of just war, and at the very moment when the balance sheet of guerrilla operations, now in course more or less everywhere in Latin America, forced many people to reflect seriously on the possibilities that this form of political struggle might still preserve, we are now witnessing a debate that is enlarging its bounds with astonishing speed and in which *the most fervent opponents of war find themselves among the most convinced defenders of violence* as the only effective means of bringing about the revolution needed to liberate the peoples of the so-called Third World.

If we limit ourselves to considering the debate now in progress from the specific point of view of the Christian conscience, inasmuch as this conscience now feels in a particularly strong way the appeal of the problems of the Third World, we immediately realize that the basic questions raised by the debate revolve around two themes—revolution and violence. Each of these two themes poses a whole series of problems and the present-day discussions, especially in Europe and in the United States, have done little more than draw them out to an infinite length.

Our purpose here is principally that of analyzing the debate on Christianity and revolution, Christianity and violence, rather than formulating our own opinions on the problems under discussion. By proceeding in this manner we hope to make some contribution to the further development of the debates.

PRESENT EXTENT OF THE DEBATE

A first analysis of the already existing bibliography on the subject of this debate immediately makes us note the fact that the greater part of the relevant literature comes from Europe and the United States. The literature coming from Latin America is to a very large extent due to European or American authors who are living there, or have lived there, or who have at least been there.

Few echoes of this debate reach us from either Africa or Asia. The debate, at least in the particular form it has taken in Europe and in the Americas, does not seem to exist there.

Latin Americans are particularly closely affected by this debate in view of the fact that Latin America is predominantly Roman Catholic and at the same time is considered to be the terrain where the problem of revolution presents itself as a most pressing one. The relative (half-hearted) participation of Latin Americans in the debate would therefore seem to require an explanation. In our opinion, this explanation may in part be due to the fact that Latin American society is still a society in which oral communication predominates. Not even the Church succeeds in escaping this fundamental law. If we were to make reference only to what is published in the form of books or reviews, it would be practically impossible to know what the topical problems of these countries are; and we would know even less about the evolution of these problems in the course of discussion and the confrontation of ideas.

Little is written, even less is published, almost nothing is preserved. In these conditions, the formation of a well-defined and operative body of concepts is practically impossible; the only result is that the most original intuitions lose themselves in an abundance of conversations and interpersonal exchanges.

On the other hand, the relative silence of the Latin Americans at a moment when "revolutionary chatter" has taken hold of such a large number of people in Europe and the United States

39

is to a very large extent due to the fact that these discussions have already taken place in Latin America and, for better or worse, have been left behind. At the present moment, pronouncements on the subject of revolution and violence are being made, above all, by the ecclesiastical authorities. Unfortunately, this is happening at a moment when the discussion "at the base" has been practically concluded and the problem of violence has been reduced to a strategic and political question, rather than a moral one.

POLITICAL AND ECONOMIC LIBERATION

At the very moment when the process of decolonization signified the appearance, the constitution of an extraordinarily large number of new states in the immense territories of the former English, French, Dutch, and Italian colonies in both Asia and Africa, another movement of even vaster proportions began to indicate what was to be the true *enjeu* of the second half of the twentieth century: the economic liberation of both the old and the new nations which, although formally independent and sovereign, are now experiencing the full weight of economic domination exercised by the ancient metropolitan states and above all, by that young imperial metropolis that Washington has become.

This domination is becoming more and more unbearable. There are many different reasons for this; we shall mention some of them.

The trading relationships between developed and underdeveloped countries are in a continuous process of degeneration; the raw materials and the agricultural products of the underdeveloped countries continue to diminish in value on the international markets, while manufactured products are continually becoming more costly for the underdeveloped importers. The efforts made by the poor countries for the purpose of achieving industrialization are being hindered and frustrated by the economic or openly political interests of the rich countries; help, assistance, and collaboration are assuming ever more the form of economic and political instruments of control and domination.

40

On the other hand, the aspirations for liberty, for greater well-being, for increased and improved consumption continue to grow among the enormous mass of the poor people of the world, to whom the media of mass communication reveal the inequalities that exist within the human family.

The elite, which traditionally retain all power in the underdeveloped countries, are showing themselves ever more incapable of finding an effective solution to the problems facing the populations they govern, and in the face of the pressures that the masses are inevitably beginning to exercise they find themselves obliged, for the purpose of defending their own position, to make common cause with the very people from whom they ought to liberate their countries. Naturally, the appearance of new elite aspiring to power for the purpose of effecting a rapid and radical transformation of those structures that maintain *ad infinitum* a situation considered to be unbearable, tends to rationalize and sharpen the already existing tensions. These are the people who introduce the concept of necessary and inevitable revolution; these are the people who are the first to discredit any possibility that the elite actually in power might have of effecting this revolution; and finally, these are the people who, when faced with the failure of attempts at "revolution in liberty," confess that they see no other effective way out than a violent assault at the seats of power.

Christianity and Revolutionary Liberation

If by revolution we understand a rapid and radical transformation of the social structures, it is at least theoretically possible to distinguish the problem of revolution from that of violence. The concept of peaceful revolution is therefore perfectly intelligible, even if a peaceful revolution were to be nothing other than a pure work of the spirit, as some people would like it to be. We propose to maintain the distinction, at least for the purposes of the discussion. Our exposition will therefore be divided into two sections, respectively dedicated to studying the relationship between Christianity and revolution, and between Christianity and violence.

41

Revolution—evolution or a clean break?

The definition of concepts is an essential prerequisite in a debate of this kind. Now, when we speak of revolution it is quite evident that not all people understand the same thing by the term. This would be almost equally true if we were to confine our examination to the most recent literature on the subject and, moreover, were to limit ourselves to authors who deal with the subject from a Christian point of view.

Almost all the representatives of the Roman Catholic hierarchy who, particularly in South America, speak of the need for a true revolution, understand revolution as a radical reform of the social structures that would have no need of violent action to be carried into effect. They therefore describe as revolution what the Pope, in *Populorum Progressio*, calls quite simply "necessary changes, indispensable reforms." [1]

In a more explicit manner, the bishops who signed the document known as "A letter from 17 bishops of the Third World" understand revolution as "a break with a system that does not ensure the common good, and the installation of a new order of things more likely to procure this common good." In this sense, therefore, the word revolution can no longer be confused with evolution. When Cardinal Samoré or Cardinal Roy, speaking of the reforms needed in Latin America, say that they prefer the term evolution to that of revolution, it is quite obvious that we are no longer concerned with a simple play on words, but rather with a substantial difference in the appraisal of the Latin American reality. We are not concerned with choosing the word evolution rather than the word revolution, but with choosing a particular type of social, economic, and political organization instead of another for the specific purpose of solving Latin America's present problems.

It would be useful to eliminate the equivocation between "revolution" and "evolution" from the debate. To prefer one term rather than the other means preferring confusion to clarity. Both terms involve the idea of change. All the same, evolution should be used to indicate changes within the limits of particular structures, while revolution should indicate a change of the structures themselves, an alteration of the system of relationships between people and groups based on a new normative scale of values. This, at least, is the differentiation proposed by the participants in "Conversations on Revolution" recently organized by *The National Catholic Reporter*, a North American Roman Catholic newspaper.[2]

We may say in a general way that the attempts to define revolution as synonymous with reform are indicative of the preoccupation not to offer the slightest foothold that might justify the use of violence.

The definition proposed by Peuchmaurd in this "Esquisse pour une théologie de la révolution" corresponds to the most common meaning of the word and aims at giving the term its full significance. He says: "By revolution we understand the brutal overthrow of an established order for the purpose of replacing it with a new order based on a new scale of values. There is a change of source, a change of the point of reference."[3]

Revolution and the Christian vision of society

If we understand the term revolution in such a way as not to involve the concept of violence, the debate on Christianity and revolution comes to be something quite pacific; little by little it ceases to be a debate and becomes a conversation.

By this we mean that the ideas of progress, of social change, of modernization, of the transformation of structures, etc., seem no longer to be in conflict with the Christian vision of society. We are undoubtedly moving further and further away from the mentality that dominated for such a long time and regarded the reformers, the innovators, the modernizers, as people to be immediately condemned. In ecclesiastical language the terms "reformer" and "modern" were infamous words. It is a paradox that Christianity, which introduced the idea of development, progress, and evolution into the history of salvation, should at the same time have preserved such a fixed and static idea of the history of human institutions.

One of the aims of the so-called theology of revolution (the term was recently disowned by the Pope in the course of his allocution to the cardinals on the 24th of June on the occasion of the anniversary of *Populorum Progressio,* although it has been accepted by the Church and Society Department of the World Council of Churches)[4] is that of destroying the preconceived theological notions which, in one way or another, serve to justify a theology of the established order.[5] Peuchmaurd, in the article we have already mentioned, lists some chapters of this theology of the established order, which is based on a concept of the creation understood as a perfect and finished work that man must preserve, on a static concept of human nature, on a static notion of tradition and on the theological justification of social hierarchies and established authorities.[6]

CHRISTIANITY AND VIOLENT LIBERATION

A discussion of revolution leads necessarily to a discussion of violence. The reason for this is quite simple. Until today, practically all the true revolutions have been effected by means of violence.

Even the pacifists and the most fervent proponents of nonviolence are perfectly agreed on this, and when they mention the example of the India of Gandhi they do so without excessive conviction. Rather than seek a justification in the past, where it is difficult to find, they look to the future and point out that nonviolence as a political instrument is not yet "sufficiently organized," as Mons. Helder Camara recently said at Paris. Nonviolence, even though it is "the very essence of the Christian message" as all nonviolent Christians seemingly maintain, can be perceived as such only when there will be a full acceptance of human values. We are now said to be living through this privileged moment. While violence has a history going back through the millennia, "nonviolence is a rather recent hypothesis" intimately linked to this acceptance, as was pointed out by Zolo on the occasion of a round table conference on revolution recently organized by *Sette Giorni.*[7]

Not all Christians profess nonviolence. Nor do all pacifists, if by that name we understand those people who condemn war as a political instrument for the resolution of conflicts between states. These pacifists-revolutionaries seem to many people to be the very incarnation of an inadmissible contradiction. Some of the people who fought to ensure that Vatican II should condemn war without any qualification and thus bury once and for all the theory of just wars, cannot accept (and even less understand) the fact that many persons or groups, who supported them in their efforts among the Council Fathers (unfortunately without any appreciable results), should now find themselves among those who justify guerrilla warfare as a revolutionary instrument. This contradiction, however, becomes less evident if one takes into consideration the motives that were adduced in support of the condemnation of war.

If this condemnation is based on the fact that modern war, as a result of technical progress, has become quite insuitable for performing the functions that it has up to now performed—because modern war tends to be a total and, above all, a nuclear war—then it can quite readily be admitted, without any contradiction at all, that revolutionary guerrilla warfare, which by its very nature does not comport the same dangers, cannot be excluded for the same reasons that call for the condemnation of war among the nations as something wholly futile. The need for avoiding a thermo-nuclear catastrophe obliges us to exclude war as an instrument of policy. But it is not by any means equally obvious that the armed struggle of a people against an established authority constitutes a menace of the same kind.

Violence in the ordinary magisterium of the church

Christians who want to reflect seriously on the subject of violence must clearly take into consideration the teachings of the ordinary magisterium of the church. Unfortunately, this magisterium cannot claim that the church has always been opposed to violence "from whatever source it may come." What causes even more apprehension is the fact that, just as the Council has once again accepted the doctrine of the just war, the ordinary magisterium seems to accept a doctrine of "legitimate violence," which might possibly be exercised by Christians against a tyrant, but which in practice constitutes an unquestioned right of established authority. In other words, the condemnation of revolution, expressed with truly vehement emphasis in the official language of the church, becomes converted into a justification of constituted authorities (unless, of course, these be Communist) even when they exercise nothing more than a legal stranglehold, as well as the most varied forms of violence, using as their instruments those selfsame social structures and institutions—such as the army, the police, and the courts—which, although theoretically created for the service of the common good, in practice function only as a means of class domination.

The official doctrine is clear only at first sight. It reserves the use of the word revolution for the purpose of indicating an abrupt and radical change effected by violent means. And, of course, it refuses such a revolution.

Populorum Progressio gives a brief but pertinent description of the conditions in which a people may find itself. In practice this is more or less what is happening in all the countries of the Third World, where injustice clamors to the heavens, where entire populations live in a state of dependence such as to be deprived of all initiative, deprived of any possibility of participating in the social, cultural, and political life of the community. In these conditions, says the encyclical,

they are sorely tempted to redress these insults to their human nature by violent means. Everyone knows, however, that revolutionary uprisings—except where there is manifest, longstanding tyranny which would do great damage to fundamental personal rights and dangerous harm to the common good of the country—engender new injustices, introduce new inequities and bring new disasters. The evil situation that exists, and it surely is evil, may not be dealt with in such a way that an even worse situation results.[8]

Violence in the practice of the church

The effective behavior of the church, however, renders this doctrine particularly opaque. In the first place, the pacifism and the nonviolence of the church are comparatively recent phenomena. For many centuries, war and violence in their most inhuman and brutal forms were the instruments of the apostolate, or at least of ecclesiastical policy. "Holy War" was a Catholic invention in the fight against the Mussulmans; anti-Semitism was a normal practice for many centuries; there were witch hunts, the most brutal concession the church ever made to superstition, and the Inquisition, a kind of Stalinism long before Stalin himself, just a little more durable. Only recently, Mons. Helder Camara pointed out (at the Brazilian College in Rome) that the Latin American church had accepted slavery of the Indians and the trade in Negroes from the very beginning. It is not sufficient consolation that throughout this history—more or less terrible, and more or less masked by official histories—we find the example of a few saints who denounced and opposed all these goings on. We advisedly say "a few saints," because we cannot possibly include all, and there were very many who justified torture and the stake.

If in the history of the church we cannot find any really concrete support for the doctrine of nonviolence as the expression of the very nature of the Gospels, it would at least have been legitimate to hope that the positions the ecclesiastic magisterium has recently taken up against war and against the use of violence as an instrument of political struggle might be wholly beyond suspicion. But there are many people, even within the church itself, who feel themselves shaken by certain attitudes and, above all, by certain official silences that seem to contradict the more explicit and formal declarations.

We are not here concerned with establishing whether such feelings are based on well-founded reasons. It is, however, of considerable interest to state clearly the most obvious implications of this opposition to violence as a political instrument.

One of these is clearly brought out by the document of the seventeen bishops of the Third World: The condemnation of the violence of the poor, "tempted," in the words of *Populorum Progressio*, "to use violence in the struggle against such grievous injuries to human dignity," must not fail to take into account the violence of the rich or simply that of the political, social, and economic structures, which they defend and sustain as the expression of social order itself. We find the following passage in the document of the seventeen bishops:

> Within each nation, too, the workers have the right and the duty to unite in real trade unions in order to claim and to defend their own rights: a fair wage, paid holidays, social security, family allowances, participation in works management. . . . It is not sufficient that the law should recognize these rights on paper. The laws must be applied and it is the duty of governments to use their powers in this field in the service of the workers and the poor. The governments must dedicate themselves to putting an end to this class struggle which, contrary to what is normally held to be the case, the rich have all too often begun and which they continue to conduct against the workers, exploiting them with inadequate wages and with inhuman working conditions. This is a subversive war, which money has been surreptitiously waging in every part of the world and for a long time, massacring entire peoples.[9]

Another point meriting particular attention is the normally adopted technique of a make-believe fight against Communism. There would seem to be no doubt that the official church favored, and particularly in Latin America still favors, a certain form of anti-Communism that ends up by unleashing the most brutal violence not only against Communists, but against all those whom the most egotistical groups choose to designate as Communists or subversives for the purpose of defending their own interests. The massacre of half a million Indonesian "Communists" did not provoke a great deal of indignation in official Roman Catholic circles. The Brazilian bishops have on innumerable occasions made public protests against the persecution, the arbitrary arrests, quite openly practiced against militant Catholic priests accused of Communism. Now, it is a cause of some worry, to say the least, that these official protests against the measures taken by the military authorities, installed in power by a manifest act of violence, always give the impression that the only reason why these measures are regarded as unjustifiable lies in the fact that they are aimed against militant Catholics. In general, it seems clear that the bishops accept, at least by implication, that the mere fact of "being a Communist," or more simply a "leftist," constitutes in itself a crime that may be punished not only in an illegal, but also in the most immoral of manners. It is therefore more necessary than ever not to forget that the church, by virtue of analogous attitudes, was for many long centuries responsible for the persecution of Jews and heretics.

Is there an alternative to violence?

If, therefore, the official doctrine of the church on the subject of revolutionary warfare, and on violence in general, is full of ambiguities, we must not be surprised to find that many Catholics reject the doctrine of nonviolence itself as being unjustifiable and even hypocritical.

One of the most frequent observations made by the representatives of this group is rather similar to the point of view expressed by Domergue in an interesting article entitled "Reflections on Violence." Here it is: "It is Pharisaic to condemn the attitude of groups or of countries who make recourse to violent means of liberation when, in fact, our own violence forced this choice upon them." [10] It was on the basis of this consideration, for example, that Camilo Torres decided in favor of armed struggle, feeling certain that he was not doing anything other than "acting in legitimate defence of the undefended."

Pastor Casalis is of the opinion that the problem of violence is frequently badly posed, and writes that "undeniably, politics are the domain of violence"; in this he is only following in the footsteps of Max Weber.[11] Casalis suggests that we should reread the twelfth chapter of the Epistle to the Romans.

In effect, it is there said that the magistrate carries the sword. I would like to try and resolve the problem over which we have stumbled so many times: violence or nonviolence? In a biblical sense, this is not even the real problem. Faulty readings of the Bible are very frequently made on this point, increasing the importance of violence. But for the Scriptures the important thing is not violence or nonviolence, or even order or disorder; what really matters are the things that make history progress in the direction of justice, the things that will be useful to living man, the weak, the exploited, the prisoner. When Paul speaks of the power that carries the sword, he says that whoever does good has no need to fear it. Nobody is called upon to love violence, but violence in the service of justice is a violence that inspires respect and fear.[12]

And was Mons. Helder Camara himself perhaps not saying the same thing when he recently declared in both Paris and Rome that, while being nonviolent by virtue of personal conviction, he had the greatest respect for Camilo Torres and Che Guevara who, choosing guerrilla warfare, had given their own lives in witness of their love for justice? [13]

Long before being a problem—and, above all, long before being a problem for the Christian conscience questioning itself as regards its significance and its legitimacy—revolution is a fact (of life). "With or without theology," observes the Dominican M. Peuchmaurd, "it develops, achieves victories, or falls into decadence." [14]

It is particularly significant that the very principle of revolution—at least understood in the sense of a profound and urgent transformation of the social structures in places where these are rightly denounced as clearly oppressive—is beginning to be admitted by an ever growing number of Christians, including bishops and priests. This is particularly true in the case of Latin America, where entire episcopal conferences have already pronounced themselves in this sense. We already have a great step forward when many Christians, including once again priests and bishops, react to the problem of violence by examining the merits of the particular case, or even clearly admit that for many oppressed people revolutionary warfare may be the only way left open to them.[15]

We should here observe that for these groups the term "oppressed people" does not necessarily mean those people who find themselves under a Communist regime, although this is almost the exclusive thought of many readers of the passage from *Populorum Progressio* that we have cited above!

The Bishop of Crateus (Brazil), Mons. Fragoso, in a recent interview published by *Informations Catholiques Internationales*, said the following in connection with his own people:

There are men who impede human advancement. I believe it necessary to establish a sincere and fraternal dialogue with them,

50

always provided that they agree to respect the reality that imposes itself. If, on the other hand, we should find that we are simply knocking our heads against a refusal to open the dialogue and against the explicit desire to squash the people, then we would have to struggle against tyranny. At times violence is the only possible way of liberating man from an established, permanent and grievous violence. We have to recognize that the mature conscience of the citizen has the right to opt for violence.[16]

The debate on the moral legitimacy of revolutionary war, or violence in general, is continually running the risk of becoming transformed into an idealistic, abstract and sterile discussion. In terms of words, nonviolence is the opposite of violence! It is not difficult to demonstrate that the message of the Gospels is a message of peace and love and not a doctrine of war and of violence! But the Gospels also carry a message of liberation. When we are considering the liberation of entire peoples, currently subjected to every kind of slavery, the end to be attained must take precedence over the means employed, and in the case under consider-
follows that the true problem for those who for religious or moral
ation these are revolutionary violence, armed insurrection. . . . It
reasons are absolutely opposed to the use of violence consists in
finding an alternative to violence, an alternative to revolutionary war. And by alternative we mean something that is realistic, possible and effective. The Protestant theologian R. Shaull [17] is currently orientating his researches in this direction, even though it is quite apparent that such a task goes well beyond the competence of theology alone.

May we be permitted to conclude with an observation that is perhaps a little inopportune. The problem that is worrying us at this time is running a considerable risk of becoming a substitute, generous only in appearance, for a real dedication which, being revolutionary in the sense of demanding profound transformations of the political, social, and mental structures at home, would have no need—or possibly would lack the conditions—for expressing itself with violence. It is to be hoped that the discussion of problems that are typically problems of the Third World will never serve to mask an evasion in the face of the problems to be found in one's own home.

Chapter Three

A Theological Perspective on Human Liberation

Richard Shaull

A number of modern historians have reminded us that the history of the West has been the history of revolution. And these revolutions have occurred not merely as the result of an objective crisis in society, but because a crisis was precipitated by the emergence and action of a new dynamic proletariat. In each case, this proletariat had been captured by a new vision of a new social order. Its members found themselves excluded from the benefits of the status quo, or repelled by its injustices. Eventually they reached a point where their consuming passion was to bring the old order down and build a new one, and they were willing to sacrifice their lives so that this could happen.

These movements became disruptive forces in their societies; in some instances, they overthrew the old order and eventually organized society on a new foundation, with new structures of economic, social, and political life. They often failed to achieve their goals, yet when we look back on our history today, we can see that many of the most significant breakthroughs toward a more human society have occurred as a result of these revolutions.

It is hard to avoid the conclusion that the emergence of such revolutionary forces is once again the order of the day. In the United States, this new proletariat has made its appearance among the black militants and the radicals of a new student generation. But it is in the Third World, and especially in Latin America, that this phenomenon is most widespread. There a vanguard, composed of men and women, old and young, of different social classes, has come to the conclusion that the total situation in which it finds itself is intolerable and must be overcome. They are convinced that the lethargy and misery of the masses, the social injustice evident everywhere, and the sclerosis of obsolete structures are due to the total order of domination created and sustained by the wedding of colonial power with the internal structures of economic and political domination by a small oligarchy. Thus, a new generation will be able to affirm its selfhood, find the road to rapid and autonomous economic development, and shape its own destiny as a nation only as this old order as a whole is overcome, and a new one is built.

In the past, the Christian Church has not done a very creative job of responding to the challenge of revolution. In some instances, it has been one of the main bulwarks of the old order; in others, it has stood on the sidelines and watched the struggle. Usually, some decades after the success of a revolution, the church has reluctantly entered into dialogue or established a *modus vivendi* with it. Must this necessarily be the case? Does the very nature of the Christian faith force us to take our stand in support of the old order? Or does it perhaps offer resources for understanding a revolutionary situation and participating in a struggle for social reconstruction? We have been forced to face this question in a very existential way in Latin America, where a new generation of Christians are now in the vanguard of the revolutionary struggle; and we would like to present, very briefly, some of the results of our theological work which was motivated by our relation with them.

THEOLOGY AND THE DIRECTION OF HISTORICAL DEVELOPMENT

It is now a generally accepted axiom that our Judeo-Christian heritage overcame the dominance of the cynical view of history. In its place, it introduced the idea that man's historical existence was gradually moving toward a goal, and that this goal was nothing less than the creation of a new humanity, a new possibility for human fulfillment within a new social order. The original Christian symbols which provided the resources for such understanding have produced a wide variety of eschatological views, often in contradiction with each other. Nevertheless, they suggest that God is at work in human history, breaking it open to a new tomorrow, and that we are best able to understand what is going on around us and respond to it when we have our eyes open to perceive new possibilities and strive to create them.

But all this is very vague. It suggests that we can look to the future with hope, but it gives us no clues as to the nature of the historical process, the shape of the new order, or how it can be brought into existence. Can we, without attempting to create some over-arching philosophy of history, say anything more specific, in theological terms, about this question? We believe that we can, especially at two points:

1. A number of theologians have suggested in recent years, that in the perspective of Christian faith, the history of man is the history of human liberation. A German sociologist, Dietrich Von Oppen, claims that the person and teachings of Christ have had a revolutionary impact on the world. He finds the clue to this revolution in Jesus' words: "The Sabbath was made for man, and not man for the Sabbath." This means, for Von Oppen, that all institutions lose their sacral, and thus authoritarian character. They exist to serve man, and thus must be seen as merely functional. To the degree that this attitude toward institutions has penetrated our culture, new structures have emerged which are open, flexible, limited in their area of influence and subject to constant critical examination; and the gradual creation of institutions of this type constitutes the context of human liberation.

A Dutch theologian, Arend Van Leeuwen, concludes that primitive societies were entirely dominated by an "ontocratic" pattern of life. By this he means that all aspects of divine and historical reality, the eternal and the temporal, were inextricably mixed together, in such a way that nature and society were sacralized. They belonged to the divine order, therefore they had authority over men and could not be tampered with. For Van Leeuwen, the Christian understanding of reality separated the divine from the created order, and thus led to the desacralizing of the world. Consequently, the growing impact of Christianity on the world has meant the gradual collapse of ontocratic structures, and this has brought increasing freedom—to man and society—to create the future. Within this framework, God's redemptive action in the world is understood as an ongoing process of human liberation. As his impact is felt, those races, classes and communities of men that have been dehumanized, move to new discoveries of human self-consciousness, new realms of experience, and thus to a new self-identity. They discover that their future is open, and that, as individuals or communities, they move toward a new stage of fulfillment as they take their destiny into their own hands and order their existence around the goals which they create. In a very interesting chapter in his book *Christianity in World History*, Van Leeuwen traces the revolutionary impact of this "virus" in our Western world across the centuries.

If this is what is going on in a world in which God is at work, we find it is hard to avoid the conclusion that we today have arrived at a climactic moment in that process. For it is this new discovery of selfhood and this new will to shape the future which is at the heart of the Negro revolution and the new stirrings among youth and students in this country, as well as the new developments in the Third World. And if this is at the center of God's action to transform and enrich human life and fill it with meaning, then we should feel ourselves closely identified with this struggle and the achievement of this goal should be our central concern as Christians at this time. In this case, our thought about Vietnam or Latin America will be determined, not primarily by the hope to see Western institutions established there, or to have change without violence, or even by the desire to "stop Communism," but rather by our concern for the struggle of emerging people as they seek the freedom to develop a new way of life for themselves.

2. The biblical story introduces a second element into our understanding of the historical process. History moves forward but it does not move upward in spirals because of the fact that time and again God's action for the liberation of man runs into difficulties. In the Old Testament, the messianic movement

toward the new order is thwarted; therefore, it can go ahead only as God tears down in order to build up. Nowhere is this more strikingly stated than in the Magnificat, where the Virgin Mary speaks of the coming of the Messiah as bringing a radical disruption of the established order. The powerful will be brought down and the humble exalted. The New Testament continues this same line, as the eschatological expectations for the future are mixed up with the apocalyptic. And as the imagery of the anti-Christ suggests, the growing influence of Christ in history leads to the union and dynamic activity of his adversaries, who have been called to life by his action. The liberating action of Christ sows the seeds of liberation in the lives of men, destroys authority of all these structures which block such liberation, and thus provokes a violent and often desperate reaction on the part of the old order.

In this context, history moves forward by leaps as the power of the old order is broken down, so that the new can emerge. It is this which leads Rosenstock-Huessey to affirm that the history of the West can only be understood as the history of revolutions. The major steps forward in the creation of new human institutions have occurred by such confrontation and struggle. And to the degree that these Christian symbols are operative in our understanding of what is going on around us, we should be prepared to recognize the importance of this element and respond creatively to the challenge it presents.

By this we mean that as Christians, we are free from the self-imposed limitations of American liberalism at this point. Nothing is more common than the affirmation that we are in favor of all efforts for the liberation of the depressed classes—as long as they do not upset too much the present system or run the risks of violence. Consequently, we are the first ones to withdraw from the struggle when it can no longer be fitted into this framework. In the perspective to which we have referred, however, the problem is seen quite differently. When the old order is no longer able to serve man adequately and is too sclerotic to change fast enough to keep up with events, it will have to be brought down or broken open by conflict and violence of one sort or another, and the dynamics of God's action in the world moves in that direction. In that situation, the violence of the struggle will be determined primarily by those in power, for it is up to them to decide whether the old can make way for the new without total confrontation and disruption. This does not justify any use of violence at any time by the agents of social change, but it does put the primary responsibility for dealing with this question where it belongs.

When we look at the world today with the biblical images in mind, we have the impression that they help us a great deal to make sense out of what we see. A new commitment to the construction of a new social order on the part of the Negro or student in this country or the new generation in the developing world is being met by tremendous efforts on the part of those in power to preserve the status quo. These new forces have rejected all relationships of paternalism on the part of the powerful, yet almost everything we do continues to express this attitude in a variety of subtle ways, as for example, when we assume that we know the solution to the problems of development of the poor nations, or that committees composed mostly of leaders of the Establishment can decide how to overcome the crisis in our urban ghettoes. The emergence of a new self-identity of many national and ethnic groups, as well as that of a new generation, is met with extraordinarily well-organized and effective pressures for conformity, which make real independence and opposition almost impossible. And the longing of the powerless for power to determine their destiny—here and abroad—is met by an expanding system of domination no longer held in check by effective countervailing power. Those in power are so bound by their past and their irrelevant ideologies, that they are no longer able to respond creatively to the demands of a new day; while those who find themselves enveloped in the shroud of the old order have the choice between the surrender of everything that has become most important for them and their society, and an arduous revolutionary struggle. Christian realism should lead us, we believe, to accept this as the context within which we define our responsibility to work for social reconstruction today.

Obviously, no one can prove that there is a God at work in history in this way. To make the wager of faith means to bet that the dynamics of history revealed at one specific moment of time and in one particular place, does indeed offer us a possibility of understanding the dynamics of the wider historical process; that the symbols and stories that make up the biblical tradition have the power to make this reality transparent to us. In Christian perspective, that which is most real cannot be grasped by mere empirical observation; it is above all the reality of the new world that is coming to be, as the future breaks into our present and makes it pregnant with new possibilities. In the language of the tradition, the action of the Triune God in history is the reality in which human life is set, and it is this which pushes man toward new possibilities of fulfillment in the midst of conflict, crisis, and social reconstruction. To live by faith is to trust that things work out that way and thus to participate in the struggle in hope.

THE CONTEXT OF PERSONAL LIBERATION

At this point, a further observation is necessary. Christian faith affirms that the Christian symbols provide us with clues to the reality of historical development and of personal existence. Jesus Christ—crucified and risen—is both the Messiah who initiates a new era in human history, and the Second Adam, the new man. The same dynamics which we perceive in the historical process are then operative in personal existence. As individuals, we move toward maturity and fulfillment in life as we allow the old to collapse and the new to arise out of death. The fact that this happens in society makes new forms of personal existence possible in the world; while the new man who is formed through daily death and resurrection can be the free agent of social reconstruction.

For this reason, we believe that the central Christian symbols for us today are those of death and resurrection. No modern thinker has stated this more powerfully than Eugen Rosenstock-Huessey, in his book, *The Christian Future*. He put it this way:

"Christianity is the embodiment of one single truth through the ages: that death precedes birth, that birth is the fruit of

58

death, and that the soul is precisely this power of transforming an end into a beginning by obeying a new name (p. 10).

In these few words we are challenged to a radical reorientation of our lives. For those who have been surprised by the irruption of the new in the midst of the old and expect to be surprised again and again on the road to the future, death can be brought into the center of life and overcome. They are free to lose their lives in the hope of finding them; to break out of the dead end of stagnation and repetition by burying the old when its time has come, and working to give form to the new. In this framework, it is possible to contemplate and accept the loss of that which we most cherish, even though we do not yet know what will take its place. The willing acceptance of the agony of creation takes the place of security within the context of old stabilities, and those who have no future or give up the future already guaranteed for them, turn out to be the ones who are free to create a new tomorrow.

If this perspective is to be transformed into a style of life, we must discover what it means to run the risk of death every day: i.e., to allow the presuppositions on which we function to be brought out into the open and called into question; to contemplate the shattering of the neat systems of thought and life in which we feel sheltered and secure; and to have the courage to start putting the pieces together once again, expecting a new design to emerge. When this happens, the Christian community becomes a parable of the coming Kingdom rather than a relic of a dead order. It is the place where we serve others by forcing them to call their thought and existence into question, where we are sustained in the time of waiting, and find the courage to risk thinking new thoughts and living experimentally.

It is hardly necessary here to mention the importance of this in relation to the situation we now face at home or in our policy toward the Third World. For the failure of American liberalism is nowhere more evident than in its inability to bury its dead. We insist in dealing with the problems of Vietnam and Latin America in terms of an international situation of two decades ago, thus ignoring the dynamics of history and the emergence of new realities. Consequently, we use our power to destroy the most creative forces of new nations and run the risks of a Third World War because we are victims of our own slogans. We have allowed ourselves to be caught in a box in which we can no longer discern the real alternatives or explore new and creative possibilities latent in the situation.

If, in the Christian community, we are able to make these resources of our heritage operative once again, something exciting could happen. It would be possible, in the midst of a dying order, to form men and women who would be free to perceive the inadequacy of old slogans, be open to new realities, develop new perspectives, and propose new alternatives. An honest look at the institutional church or at the witness of history is not likely to give us much hope for this to happen in the church as a whole. But it may well be that here and there small communities can arise that will meet this challenge in creative ways.

The Church and the Struggle for Liberation in Latin America

If this interpretation of the meaning of our Christian heritage is legitimate, it could well revolutionize our perspective on Latin America and lead us to a commitment to a new struggle there as well as in this country. If we are free to understand what is involved in the struggle for liberation in Latin America today, then our own responsibility will be sharply redefined. To my mind, the most significant work on this has been done by Professor Candido Mendes, of Brazil, whose participation in CICOP and other international Catholic movements, is well known to many. Professor Mendes contends that underdevelopment is not simply a lack of certain resources and techniques; it is a *total social* fact, which is the product of the structures of society and patterns of relationship with the outside world that developed during the colonial era. Each country was used as a source of raw materials and as a market for the products of the metropolis, and its social structures were shaped by this fact. The economic order was based on the large landowners in the country and the merchants in the city. The political system was the instrument by which this very small ruling class distributed patronage and developed a clientele. The masses were submerged in a state of lethargy; there was no independent middle class; and this intellectual and cultural life of the elite was oriented toward the metropolis.

In this context, according to Candido Mendes, national emancipation and economic development depend upon overcoming this total situation of the past. This involves the integration of the nation around nationalist goals, comprehensive economic planning moving in the direction of socialism, together with the control and disciplined use of the economic resources available, intensive efforts to awaken the masses for full participation in creating a new society, and the encouragement of a new generation of leadership oriented toward national emancipation and development. In other words, this can mean nothing less than the end of the old order and the creation of new social, economic, and political structures which can serve the goals of national development. It inevitably means a radically changed relationship with the United States, because national development, by its very nature, requires that the new nations find their own solutions to their problems, build the structures most adequate for their situation, and be as independent as possible of outside economic domination.

A new generation in Latin America understands this and is committed to working for it in these terms. In recent years, especially among Catholic youth, extraordinary things have been happening, as they have thrown themselves into the struggle for development at many points, and worked at building a new political base for the creation of a new social order. But in many instances, their experience has been terribly frustrating, for they have discovered that the small ruling elites that are unable to take the initiative in social reconstruction and economic development, are nevertheless willing to pay any price to remain in power and preserve their privileges. And what is even more disastrous, these Catholic young people have become convinced that the use of United States power—economic, political, and military—is the major force sustaining the old order and blocking

61

the creation of a new one. The end result is very clear. For an increasing number of these people, there is only one hope: the organization of armed movements of national liberation, with all the sacrifice and bloodshed that it involves. In recent months, we have been amazed to discover how many groups of Catholics and Protestants have moved to this conclusion, after all their efforts to work for change by political means had been systematically destroyed.

These events confront all of us in the church with a new call for decision. In the past, the church has often been the bulwark of the status quo, or stood on the sidelines while the fight for a new society was going on. Fortunately, our awareness today of our Christian responsibility for economic development and national emancipation has pushed us beyond that point. Yet we suspect that for most of us, reliance on guerrilla warfare is not an attractive prospect. We are rightly horrified by the price this would demand, in bloodshed, the sacrifice of a new generation, and the long delay in urgent steps toward development.

But do we have any alternative to offer? The only possibility we see is if Christians and the Church could become a catalytic force in the development of a new type of opposition to the present trend and power structures. This would mean accepting all the risks involved in creating pressure groups that would try to break the situation open; confront the present forms of domination; insist on freedom to build the political power of peasants, workers, and students; and support students, labor leaders, intellectuals, and priests who are now working to build a new order. This would not be an easy or a pleasant task; it might not have much chance to succeed. But it could open the possibility for a rebirth of hope in the political struggle for social reconstruction and we can think of nothing that would be more important in Latin America at this time.

Those of us who remain in the United States have an even more difficult task. If we are concerned about the future of Latin America, the important thing for most of us is not for us to go there but to remain here and accept the responsibility for a long-term struggle to change a society which by its own inner logic, has become the enemy of movements of human liberation in the Third World—and here at home. And to change our policy toward that part of the world is not something that can be done by lobbying in Washington or pressing for more economic aid. It requires nothing less than a radical critique of our society, the development of a new basis of political power for radical change, and the gradual formation of a new public opinion on foreign policy. Only as these things happen can we hope, as a nation, to be sympathetic with and support the new forces in Latin America, encourage and permit them to develop the economic and political structures most adequate to their situation, and control the way in which United States private capital operates abroad.

Very few instruments now exist for doing this, so that today our most urgent task may be to work with other radicals in our society toward the creation of such small communities, willing to attack one or another of these problems on a long-term basis. In the past we have encouraged priests, nuns, and laymen to serve the people of the Third World by giving their lives to missionary communities in these lands. Whatever the importance of this task may still be, we now face a new challenge: to encourage this type of commitment to communities in this country that are trying to serve the rest of the world by means of intense intellectual and political efforts to transform our society, and its structure of relations to other nations. We know of one group of twelve young people related to the North American Congress on Latin America (NACLA) who have formed such a team to work on the analysis and exposure of how United States power now operates in Latin America. To do this, they are living on a subsistence basis in New York, most of them taking part-time jobs in order to support themselves as they work at this task. We see this as only one small example of the type of communities now needed to work on a variety of issues in the university, in relation to church groups, in suburbia, and on many other fronts. Nothing less than this, we believe, will be adequate for the challenge now confronting us when we take seriously our responsibility as Christians in the contemporary struggle for human liberation.

Chapter Four Why the Gospels Are Revolutionary: The Foundation of a Theology in the Service of Social Revolutions

Vitaly Borovoj

I intend no more here than simply to bear witness to the living truth that characterizes the church to which I belong, the Russian Orthodox Church. I know that the theme of this essay is being faced by Christians in different ways; and this is a sign of the strength and the validity of Christian engagement; but it is also a sign of weakness and insufficiency; but Christian truth, which by its very nature is one and indivisible, finds diverse and multiple expression in life and in the conscience of men. My own contribution may therefore well have a precipitous character and some characteristics peculiar to itself. But I dare to say that I feel myself to be particularly competent as regards this subject, because I study it from the point of view of the Russian Orthodox Church and this church has lived for half a century in the conditions of the social revolution that is the basis of almost all the social revolutions of our time. In this respect I do not think that anybody will be able to contest that we know what we are talking about. In fact, it is one thing to give a theoretical description of the role of theology in a time of social revolution or to participate in an academic discussion of this subject while being comfortably seated in an armchair near the fireplace in the serene atmosphere of a library; but it is quite a different thing to live in the conditions created by a social revolution, and personally to have the experience of what it means to indulge in theology and live a life bearing witness to Christ in the midst of a socialist and secularized society.

I am of the opinion that the impartial judgment of history

authorizes us to say that our Church has passed the test with success, a test that examined its competence in the subject that interests us at this moment, a test that lasted for almost fifty years and we can say that through the life and the testimony of its faithful members it has demonstrated how theology acts on the social revolutions of our times.

FORGETTING THE PAST AND LOOKING TOWARD THE NEW

First of all, it is essential to clarify the sense in which the two principal terms of our subject are to be understood: "revolution" and "theology of revolution." A heavy atmosphere of dangerous ambiguity has for a long time surrounded the word "revolution"; it has been used differently in too many cases and it has been too readily abused for different and at times contradictory purposes. Many Christians fear the word and prefer to avoid it altogether, or only make use of it to indicate a phenomenon of which they disapprove. But this is clearly an unrealistic attitude. The word has become too common, it has become too much a part of contemporary man for abolishing it with a single stroke of the pen or for attributing it but one meaning, i.e., a negative and anti-Christian meaning. On the other hand, there are many Christians who use the word quite willingly to indicate the simple and gradual evolution toward a new society, without this necessitating a radical break with the past. But let us consider revolution in the wider sociological meaning of the term; revolution is a total break, the overturning of relationships, the transformation of life, and then a reconstruction. In a more organic sense it is a renewal, a regeneration, a new life.

We speak of technical revolution, of the revolution of language, morals and of daily life during the last few centuries; but we also speak of the revolution that Christianity has caused in the world. We shall readily note that there is a variety of shadings in this acceptance of the term; we are here accumulating mechanical, organic and spiritual meanings on the world revolution.

On the other hand, all these revolutionary initiatives differ from one another by their degree of sharpness, by the rapidity of their development and by the violence of the break with the past. The essential fact is the radical renewal, the new life that does not want to continue the life of the past, but which intends to be free to move forward to the future. Let us therefore take revolution in its widest meaning, let us apply it to all fields of cultural, political and social life, and then let us ask ourselves what is the relationship between Christianity and revolution.

In my opinion, there should be no doubt at all as regards the answer: renewal, new and always totally different life are fundamentally Christian notions. The ancient world lived in the idea of a perfect circle, of an eternal return and the subordination of being to the laws of nature. Christianity has in a certain sense declared war on the "natural" life because it is contaminated with sin, and calls upon man to submit to a completely new and supernatural order: the Kingdom. But at the threshold of this Kingdom it requires conversion. "Repent, because the Kingdom of Heaven draws nigh." According to the Greek *meta-voeite*, "to repent" means to change spirit, to be spiritually reborn. The "birth through the Spirit" of the Gospel according to John is an even stronger ontological expression to indicate this fact.

The conversion of saints like Paul and Augustine, or those of numerous ascetics, are the proof of a spiritual revolution brought about by the discovery of a higher and more noble type of man in Christianity. The Christian life begins with a crisis and continues in a state of crisis. Conversion is not a unique act, but rather a permanent state. The power of sin is not abolished with a single stroke; incessant efforts and continually renewed abnegations are needed. One continually has to break with the force of evil, carry through spiritual revolutions and change direction.

The direction towards which Christianity is tending is forward and up, as Paul says in his well-known text: "Forgetting what is behind me and throwing myself towards what lies ahead" (Philippians 3:13).

A Radical and Global Renewal

What I have said above is readily accepted at an individual level. But what seems really strange is the fact that as soon as one faces up to the problem of social renewal, Christians begin to seek a way out, to refuse their responsibilities and to fight in defense of social sin, at times even openly; and all this for no other reason than the simple fact that an evil that has existed for centuries and even for millennia has acquired the pleasing patina of antiquity and tradition.

Among all the Christian civilizations, Byzantinism has possibly contributed more than any other to sanctifying social evil; it accepted without any objection the entire social heredity of the pagan world and conferred the sacral unction upon it. The civil law of the pagan Roman Empire was preserved for more than a thousand years in the guise of ecclesiastic tradition in Byzantium and medieval Europe, and for several centuries also in Russia, starting from the epoch (the 16th century) when our country began to consider itself the heir of Byzantium.

But this is radically opposed to the social tradition of primitive Christianity and the Greek Fathers, to the missionary preaching of our Savior and to the entire content of the teaching of the Old Testament prophets. The religion revealed in Israel and the Church of the early days were above all revolutionary; only later did it become individualistic and static. The Kingdom of God was the reign of the people of God before it became the reign of the soul of each individual.

Our own epoch is called upon to establish an equilibrium between the personal and the social effects of Christianity. It is a sin to abandon oneself to one's own psychosomatic nature; but it is also a sin to bend one's knee in front of social evil and injustice.

The concept of conversion, i.e., a radical change of mentality, a radical break with one's former way of life, a radical repudiation of ancient and sinful usages, an equally radical acceptance of oneself, a dedication of the whole of one's being to a new and perfect life, in other words everything that we understand by revolution, must be applied not only to the individual, but also the whole of society, to the nation, to the class, to every social group.

Conversion is a calling to a renewal, to revolution, to a new life, and it is a calling that is directed to each individual separately and to society as a whole. Christianity is thus revolutionary by its very nature; and the new road required by Christian social ethics is more radical, more profoundly revolutionary and more original than any other system, or any other doctrine that has come into being outside Christianity.

The traditional nature of Christianity and its respect for tradition should signify fidelity to good traditions, not to bad traditions. The revision of Christian values is always to be applied to relative values and must not touch absolute principles. Idolatry of the new at all costs is quite alien to Christianity. We are in favor of the new if it is better than the old; but it would be even more exact to say that Christians are neither for the new nor the old, but for the eternal.

And yet, the eternal can never become incarnate in the temporal except through the eternal creation of new forms that transform themselves into new qualities, through a continual renewal of new forms, through revolution. But if Christianity is revolutionary by nature and if the primitive Christian communities were social in the structure of their life and in their teaching, the situation becomes completely different as soon as we consider theology as a system and the Church as a historical institution. Systematic theology and the historical Churches have never been part of a revolution, and this for the simple reason that they have been prisoners of a cosmocentric vision of reality, prisoners of a static vision of a social order established once and for all upon the earth.

In fact, it has only been possible to elaborate a theology of development and revolution during the last few decades; this is due to the fact that this period has seen the most profound changes in philosophical, scientific, and theological thought, a kind of revolution caused by the anthropocentric vision of the universe and by the revision of the values of the entire history of mankind.

Although the efforts made in the revolutionary sense are rather recent, they nevertheless imply a return to the Bible and, more particularly, to the Gospels of primitive Christianity. In this context, the new theology of revolution and development has overturned the old concepts of the sacred nature of the status quo as being fundamentally opposed to the biblical message of God who revolutionizes history through the incarnation of the Logos, through the joys of Easter, the triumph over evil, through the Church of the incarnate Word, through the sanctification of each man and all things by the Spirit, thus leading humanity towards the creation of the Kingdom of God.

Bearing all this in mind, how can Christians consider it right to remain outside the revolutionary processes of history and mankind. Catholic, Protestant and Orthodox theology have already done a great deal of work on this problem; among the Catholics it is enough to make particular mention of E. Mounier, among the Protestants, Lehmann and Shaull, and Exemplarsky and Titlinov among the Orthodox. The ecumenical movement as a whole and more particularly the Ecumenical Council, just as the Vatican II Council for the Catholic Church, are the best witnesses of a recognition of the necessity, the requirements and the fundamental objectives of a theology in the service of the social revolution of our times.

And yet, these attempts are nothing other than a starting point, a simple experiment with an as yet uncertain outcome.

THE RUSSIAN CHURCH: A MUCH-DISCUSSED, BUT CONCRETE EXAMPLE

The experiences of the life of our Russian Orthodox Church, lived in the framework of a completely secularized socialist society that is the result of what is possibly the greatest social revolution of all time, could not only be an enrichment of every other Christian experience, but also a reference point for our Christian brethren in the West. It is quite essential nowadays that all Christians should take account of the experience of our church in their relationships with the social revolutions of our epoch. Our church, in the person of its hierarchy and a part of its clergy, passed through all the stages of refusal, of opposition and even direct action against the revolution and the changes that it brought in the life of the church. This was not a case of a theoretical refusal or a passive resistance; but rather a bitter and open fight. The outcome for the church was the loss of millions of believers. When the revolution had already started, and also during its subsequent evolutionary processes, large numbers of the revolutionary intelligentsia, the workers and the young people abandoned the church and broke off every relationship with Christianity. The victorious revolution moved forward on the difficult road of consolidation and development without the church.

But it so happened that the great majority of the mass of believers who remained faithful to Christianity and the church, those whom we call the "People of God," had in the meantime become a constituent element of the new society founded on the basis of the revolution; these faithful thus became an example for the clergy and the hierarchy who had refused to accept the revolution. And this fact has helped the whole of our clergy and our hierarchy to unite their fate to the life of the people and to accept what by now had become accomplished fact. Our brothers in the West should learn an important lesson for themselves from these concrete facts.

Christians should associate themselves courageously, honorably and actively with the new life based on social justice; they should bring Christian fervor to the social revolutions of our time and thus avoid the de-Christianization of the contemporary world. And such an engagement will not remain without effect on the very nature of the social revolution.

The theology of development and revolution, new in its biblical form and its content, will have a positive influence on the course of history and on the thought of the new revolutionary and socialist societies. This theology can and must raise a whole series of new questions regarding the supreme sense of the world and its evolution, manifesting by its words and its actions everything that is good, authentic, eternal and absolute in biblical Christianity as it was revealed by God. And this could help the social revolution of our epoch to lead man to his fulfillment and his fullness.

This form of stimulus, this engagement of theology in the revolutions of our times, is not just a long-term possibility; the experience of our Russian Orthodox Church shows that it can be a very real fact. The very existence of our Church and its millions of believers, who are active constructors of socialism, imposes upon secular society the duty of rethinking the role and the importance of Christianity for the future; because God has said: "I am the way, the truth and the life. . . . Without me you can do nothing . . ." In this lies our hope and our faith regarding the future of the Church in our epoch of social revolutions.

Part II The Confrontation of the
Great Revolutionary Forces

Chapter Five   Christianity and the Socialist Revolution

J. M. Gonzalez-Ruis

When we speak of the Christian's attitude in the face of revolution, we naturally have in mind the social, economic and political revolution that is called for by a profound and seriously socialist driving force. Our first task will therefore be quite simply that of clarifying the nature of such a revolution in its most essential and universal aspects. In the first place we take the term "revolution" to mean the passage of state power from one class to another. It does not mean the passage of power from one individual to another, while the objective situation remains as before. This would not be a true change of the guard.

Nor can we say that every passage of power from one class to another constitutes a true revolution; it can, in fact, quite easily be the case that the new class taking over the reins of power has the same degree of decadence as the displaced class. In such a case we are dealing with a counter-revolution. It is therefore an essential precondition that the new class in power should be a rising class, a revolutionary class, capable of creating new structures, and overcoming the decadence of the defeated groups.

Furthermore, it is not sufficient to destroy the decadent class; the new class must necessarily be ready and capable of efficiently creating the new order it is intended to establish. This means that one must patiently create the objective conditions that make possible the birth and maturation of the new class, so that it may be ready to shape history in the true sense of the term.

75

These objective situations of revolutionary maturation cannot be obtained by means of reforms and special concessions granted by the dominant classes. That would be reformism or revisionism. If a revolution is truly necessary, then the structural mechanism is corrupt to the core: and such a basic corruptness cannot be overcome with little reforms that do not reach down to the deeper reality of things. An authentic revolution is an opening and not just a miserable little crack.

In the case of the socialist revolution, capitalism intends to survive by making concessions to the working class for the purpose of prolonging its own existence. In this sense reformism and revisionism are the worst enemies of an authentic revolution; each authentic product finds its most dangerous competitor in the substitute material that seems to resemble it. The false socialists of the right wing, in fact, have very well understood this need for offering excellent pseudo-revolutionary products on the market. Thus H. Laski, an English "socialist," writes the following: "Historically there is only one reply to the menace of revolution: to carry out the reforms which will give hope and courage to those people to whom the revolutionaries would otherwise appeal with quite irresistible claims." [1]

If we then come to examine the concrete aspects of the socialist revolution, we are bound to say that it distinguishes itself from all others inasmuch as these latter merely reduced themselves to substituting one form of exploitation for another. The task of the socialist revolution, on the other hand, does not limit itself to changing the form of exploitation, but rather intends to eliminate exploitation altogether. The means by which it proposes to attain this goal is that of making class differences disappear from human society. In other words, because the working class is also the exploited class, it is the only one that can carry this struggle to completion. The working class must take in hand the reins of the rising current of history. In this manner the proletariat comes to the forefront of the stage of the human adventure.

Violence is not strictly necessary in order to achieve this victory, although there must be effectiveness. Even the strictest socialist, or better, Communist orthodoxy does not postulate violence as something that is *a priori* unavoidable. The Marxist-Leninist classics frequently emphasize that the proletariat would prefer to take power peacefully in order to transform capitalist society into a Communist one. The working class, they say, has a great interest in seeing that the revolution develops in a peaceful manner, because this way reduces the number of victims and makes it possible to avoid the destruction of means of production that is the inevitable result of every civil war. If, by chance, the working class finds itself compelled to have recourse to the force of arms, this is due to the resistance of the exploiting classes who are the first to make use of violent repression.

These are the essential aspects of the socialist revolution in the strictest sense of the term as they are expounded by the classics of socialism in general, and by Marxism-Leninism in particular. It will now be our task to examine those principles and more particularly this practice, in the light of the Christian message, taking the Bible itself as our starting point and also taking into account the ideological attitude of the Church.

THE CHRISTIAN FACED BY THE CHOICE BETWEEN CAPITALISM AND SOCIALISM

Capitalism as a socio-economic and political structure is defined by the four laws that have governed its economic evolution and transformation. The first and foremost of these laws is the search for a profit. The capitalist economy is a market economy, that is to say, production is not undertaken in order to satisfy the immediate needs of the producer, but rather to be put on the market. And this scope of selling on the market is not pursued for the purpose of rendering a service to humanity, but in order to achieve a gain, which is called profit. The search for a profit is the true purpose of capitalist enterprise. Profit is therefore the motor of the capitalist economy.

Three other laws must be added to this fundamental law of profit: the competition between capitalists themselves for the purpose of achieving better sales of their products, the concentration of the means of production, and of production itself, in the hands of an increasingly small number of capitalists, and lastly the progressive reduction of the rate of profit in order to ensure overcoming the competitors. When seen in its essence, which has been very summarily described, capitalism must be considered by Christian morality as something that is intrinsically perverse in its structure. Christian morality is a morality of loving one's neighbor, whereas capitalism arises structurally from the search for a profit. In a capitalist society it is impossible to imagine a true Church of Christ, unless it be in a missionary state. Its true task would be that of prophetic denunciation: this is a society that is wholly in a state of sin, structurally invaded as it is by egoism as the supreme driving force of its dynamics of expansion.

The existence of the Church within a capitalist society carries within itself the seeds of apostasy with respect to the Gospels. We cannot deny that within the shadow of this capitalist environment there has come into being and has developed a pseudo-theological practice, which considers the sole task of the Church to be the salvation of souls, and this understood in a spiritual and angelic sense of absolute evasion. Marx's critique of religion is conceived in this very context: the exploiting group in capitalist society finds a magnificent ally in religion, because the salvation promised by religion would always be an individual salvation; instead of trying to help his brethren to lift themselves out of their misery, the believer takes comfort in the Christian egoism of salvation, and is concerned only with the well-being of his own soul.[2] If one could speak of a "biblical anthropology," one would have to say that it brings the whole of man to the foreground. The Bible has an interest in historical man, a concrete interest in material man. It was the Bible that introduced into human culture the sense of the linear and unitarian history of a design. And this design is essentially bound up with the evolution of the material. One could therefore speak of a certain "biblical materialism," whose supreme expression is to be found in the faith in bodily resurrection.

Reading the Pauline Epistles, and above all the fifteenth chapter of the First Letter to the Corinthians, brings out the most essential role of bodily resurrection in primitive Christian mystique. Or rather, in this so-called Christian mystique, which has been in fashion during these last few centuries, resurrection hardly finds a place; there are moments when the believer seriously begins to ask himself what may be the purpose of the resurrection of bodies, since the soul is considered as the only important reality of the human whole. Nevertheless, Saint Paul categorically asserts that faith in Christ would have no sense without faith in resurrection, it would be an authentic alienation.

In other words, the spiritualization of Christian soteriology is a perversion of the evangelical message regarding man; and it cannot be denied that the existence of the Church in a capitalist society has strongly conditioned the mentality of Christians, turning them into conformists and evaders. The "bosses" of this society have instinctively exploited this perversion, which rendered them services that were anything but negligible.

We might therefore speak of a typically capitalist heresy: excessive attention to the spirit and the individual, neglecting the body and its part in a history that is dialectically dynamic history and closely linked to a material evolution.

In this way one can understand why capital is offered so readily for the great cultural and liturgical undertakings. A sumptuous and rich cult creates a kind of spiritual drunkenness, which serves as a stabilizing climate for the situation created by the "bosses." For us Catholics, the Vatican II Council has made a great leap, reestablishing its links with the purer biblical anthropology. In several places it is clearly stated that "eschatological hopes do not diminish the importance of temporal tasks, but rather bring further motives for carrying them out." [3] And even more clearly:

Christians err when, on the pretext that we have no permanent abode here, they believe that they can neglect pastoral tasks; Christians of this kind do not realize that their own faith is a motive that forces them to a more perfect fulfillment of all these tasks, according to the personal vocation of each individual. But no less serious is the error of those who believe that they can dedicate themselves wholly to temporal affairs, as if these were completely estranged from a

79

religious life, thinking that this latter reduces itself to certain ritual acts and the fulfillment of certain moral obligations.[4]

As a conclusion drawn from these summary considerations, one might say that a truly evangelical Church cannot tie itself structurally to a society of the capitalist type; it can only insert itself in the human community of such a society by assuming its true prophetic role, i.e., an attitude of habitual denunciation of the system that gives birth to this society and holds it together.

We have a clear parallel in the history of primitive Christianity. The Christians found themselves face to face with a pyramidal society. The apex of this pyramid was occupied by a "boss," who arrogated unto himself the title of "lord." This title had a sacred resonance, and in fact the "boss" became a "god" for his subjects. The Christians obstinately refused to attribute the title of "lord" to the "boss" of Roman society. The Christian shout of the martyrs *"Kyrios Christos"* (Christ is our Lord) was the reply to the roar of the crowd acclaiming the "boss" with *"Kyrios Kaiser"* (Caesar is our lord). This was not merely a question of words; behind the acclamation there was a whole political attitude, which the Christians considered to be immoral. We can therefore readily understand why the defence of the Roman Empire against the Christian rebels was an altogether reasonable act if one's starting point is represented by the constitutional principles of that society, which we might describe as based on "seigneurial or despotic exploitation."

In a similar manner, today's Christians should consider themselves to be strangers in the midst of capitalist society, where the god "profit" reigns everywhere supreme. It follows that the evangelization of the human community inserted in the world of capital cannot be achieved on the basis of pacts and concordats with capital itself, but only by assuming an attitude of habitual denunciation of the egoistic structure that brings this society into being. The history of Constantine has been repeated in the modern epoch; Constantinism was the result of inserting the Church in the power structure and making it part and parcel of this self-same power. Neo-Constantinism has come about by inserting the Church in the structure of capital, which she is offered for the purpose of financing evangelization.

In this manner the word of God is being enchained by the strong fetters of financial interests. This is the tragedy of our Roman Catholic Church in many occidental countries. The pastors often lose consciousness of their prophetic role and sleep quietly in the sweet drunkenness of a cult financed by the great bosses of capital, who squeeze the church with the golden fetters of their splendid alms. Our Christian hands have lost their evangelical sensitivity and no longer get scorched as they receive the diabolical gold of the "most Christian" exploiters of our society.

In fact, the only alternative to capitalism today is represented by socialism. For the purpose of defining the attitude of Christians in respect to socialism, we intend this term in its widest meaning, but shall take it to be concretely expressed by truly scientific socialism and not by the utopian variety. This latter is distinguished by an excess of good will, but is very far from being an objective, serious and scientific analysis of the causes that have brought the capitalistic structure into being and of the methods that might be suitable for replacing it with a truly socialistic structure, i.e., a society where exploitation becomes "structurally" impossible. In the conciliar constitution on the church in the world of today, the Catholic Church has taken up a clear position in favor of this scientific road to socialism:

> Development must remain under the control of man. It must not stay in the hands of a few people or of some economically powerful groups, nor in the hands of a single political community, or even in the hands of certain powerful nations. On the contrary, at every level the largest possible number of people, and all the nations on the international plane, *should* take an active part in the orientation of development.[5]

Naturally, the church does not propose a technical solution that should lead to this goal, but gives free rein to men so that they should find the most suitable means for socializing the politico-economic structure. In other words, the church does not propose a "Catholic Road to Socialism," but for the first time in its modern history it has foregone creating a "Christian type" corresponding to the human type prevailing in contemporary society. And again, we may say that when the church, at a not so very distant date, became reconciled to democracy, it pulled out of its sleeve its own version of democracy: Christian democracy. The Vatican II Council has been a great step forward; the church, linking itself once again to its principles, has certainly reconciled itself with socialism but has openly foregone creating its own kind of socialism, a Christian socialism. The attitude of the church is that of giving free rein to Christians so that they may create the road that will most effectively lead to this goal of overcoming the structure of "institutionalized exploitation," that is to say, capitalism itself.

In truth, certain attempts that have been made to create a Christian socialism have fallen into well-merited discredit. One must honestly recognize the truth of Marx's criticism of attempts of this kind:

Nothing is easier than giving a socialist hue to Christian asceticism. Is it perhaps not true that Christianity also opposed private property, marriage and the state? And is it not perhaps true that in their place it has preached charity and poverty, celibacy and the mortification of the flesh, the monastic life and the Church? Christian socialism is nothing other than the holy water with which the priest blesses the challenge of the aristocracy.[6]

Certainly, Marx's criticism is exaggerated, and in this excessively simplified form it is not today shared by the best Marxist thinkers, especially the French and Italian ones. But the basis of the problem remains intact and more than valid even to this day: Christianity is only a religion, and not a humanism. This does not mean that Christianity neglects the humanizing task that weighs upon the shoulders of every member of our race. Once again, the Vatican II Council has succeeded in finding the precise expression: "The mission of the church is a religious one, and for this very reason it is entirely human." [7]

What then will be the Church's specific contribution to the revolutionary construction of socialism? Fundamentally its task reduces itself to rendering, through its faithful believers, a testi-

mony regarding the ethics and the mystique of universal brotherhood and love of one's neighbor, and this will very positively
condition the socializing practice. It is a pity that in the great
home of socialism, the Soviet Union, the best exponents of the
new Christian ethical thought, which is decidedly socializing,
should still be treated with so much superficiality. And thus we
find the following miserable description of "Christian personal-
ism" in the volume *Fundamentals of Marxist Philosophy*:

> Personalism is currently being practiced in the United States with
> R. F. Flewell and W. E. Hocking, in France with Emmanuel
> Mounier, and also in some other capitalist countries. From the point
> of view of personalism, the universe is a gerarchic order of persons;
> all natural bodies, all living beings, man himself, are persons, and
> lastly God is an absolute person. In proclaiming the principle of
> individuality as a cosmic principle, the personalists declare that
> "human rights," the assertion of the human personality and the liberty
> of man constitute the foundation stone of existence. Nevertheless, all
> these declarations are nothing more than a show window, behind
> which a diametrically opposed content is hidden; because in reality
> the personalist philosophers propagate and sanction slavery and the
> humiliation of the human personality, because they put the will of
> God above the individual, the will of the "divine person," of whom
> the concrete and real person is nothing but a reflection.[8]

One cannot judge a man like Mounier with so much injustice, because he made such cutting assertions as the following:
"Revolutionary means simply, but truthfully, that the disorder of
this century is too deep rooted and too obstinate to be eliminated
without spilling something, without a profound revision of values, a reorganization of the elite." And again: "To speak of revolution of our industrial era, and to think that this revolution will
be made without the working class acting as its spearhead, is a
puerile notion that is only believed by political ambition or the
ingenuity of some obtuse minds." [9]

Mounier has been a "clairvoyant" prophet of the new political expression of the new Christian ethic. In *The Agony of
Christianity* he wrote:

> Some people are not far from identifying the revolution with the
> Kingdom of God, just as their forefathers confused monarchy with

theocentrism, and the bourgeois order with the Christian order. Any new order is potentially an established order. Any form of anti-Phariseeism carries within itself the seeds of a new kind of Phariseeism. Christianity is not by any means interested in replacing the conformism of the right with a conformism of the left, in replacing conservative clericalism with revolutionary clericalism, in drowning a necessary revolution in a philanthropic religiousness which would weaken the revolutionary action and at the same time would prostitute religion.[10]

THE CHRISTIAN AND THE CLASS STRUGGLE

The problem that concerns us is limited to the class struggle in the strictest sense of the word, the struggle between the proletariat and the bourgeoisie. In this struggle the proletariat is conscious of its historical destiny; it is the protagonist of this struggle. The purpose of this struggle is the disappearance of any kind of exploiting social class; its aim is not only a change of the guard, but rather a reversal of the socio-economic situation of capitalism.

The moral aspect of the class struggle is one of the great points of attrition between Christianity and socialism. The first and greatest reproach that socialists and Communists make against Christianity is that it blesses the division of the classes and stabilizes it with the advice of resignation it gives to the poor and the advice of "charity" it gives to the rich, offering both of them a compensation in the life beyond.

We don't want to waste much time in taking the bull by the horns. Our starting point is a humble recognition that this fact has debased our Christian history; and we must confess that in doing so Christians were wrong as Christians.

In the first place, the appearance of Christianity presented itself as something truly revolutionary. The Pauline cry "There shall be neither slave nor master" (Galatians 3:28) must be understood in its true historic context. It is quite useless to pretend that Paul was only thinking of a purely spiritual and religious equality while leaving the social inequality wholly intact. Above all, Paul's biblical mentality did not permit him to "disintegrate" man; rather, as we have already seen, the material dimension of man was an essential part of Paul's soteriological anthropology.

Furthermore, in the environment of the times, within which Paul lived, there was a very close link between religious and social attitude. The temples of the free were not open to the slaves; for slaves and masters to unite in the same sacred place and to participate in the same ceremony was in itself a powerful seed of social upheaval.

In chapter two of the First Letter to the Corinthians, Paul reproaches the rich with having introduced socio-economic divisions into the eucharistic assembly, and these divided rich Christians and poor ones from the very start. Liturgical participation in the same bread and the same wine is already the beginning of the overcoming of the social division prophetically denounced by the Apostle in his great revolutionary cry. He therefore gives the following fundamental rule for those who come to the sacred rite: "Give value to the body of the Lord." In other words, give it its true value as the cement of the community of the faithful; thus, if a Christian community continues to have social divisions within itself (slaves and masters), it means that it "becomes responsible for the body and the blood of the Lord."

Then, in a second moment, came the practical aspects. This structural division could not be overthrown in a brief moment. The evolutionary process of that society was very slow indeed, Christianity was not a revolutionary technique, but rather a religious mystique that provided the impetus for the faithful to dedicate themselves to effective movements for overcoming the division of the classes. Thus it can be understood why Paul and the other writers of the first Christian generation gave advice that was seemingly in contradiction with the revolutionary impetus of this great cry. But even this occasional advice contains within itself the seed for overcoming this situation of division. One only has to read Paul's marvelous letter to the Christian "master" Philemon, consigning him his old slave Onesimus. One must never forget this dialectic between the principles and the fatal reality. The Church has fallen into the great temptation of elevating to the rank of principles those practical evangelical counsels that one must necessarily give in those moments when the revolutionary impetus of history suffers a fatal stagnation.

Marxists have never ceased to recognize a robust revolutionary germ in the Christian faith. R. Garaudy has recently put into relief the fact that the whole history of the Church is characterized by an internal dialectic, which moves between two poles: the Constantinian pole and the apocalyptic pole. "I would prefer to call this latter the 'prophetic pole.'" [11]

Let us sum up. It is not orthodox to say that Christianity as such supposes a stabilization of the disorder established by the dishuman division of society into two fundamental classes, the class of oppressors and the class of the oppressed. Every time that Christianity acts in this stabilizing manner it betrays the most essential part of its message.

The second point of friction in the problem of the class struggle is provided by the concept of "struggle" itself. This is a word that frightens many Christian ears, which nevertheless are very used to the word "crusade." The struggle of the proletariat, aimed at overcoming a society divided into classes, can take place along a peaceful road.

But there are moments in which a peaceful life becomes impossible and it is then that one must have recourse to violence. And this immediately brings us to our question: is there some brake that prevents a faithful Christian from participating in this struggle, and particularly in its violent aspect?

In order to reply to this question one only has to seek the classical principles of Christian morality with regard to the right of self-defence against an unjust aggressor. In a capitalist society of today there is a permanent unjust aggressor constituted by the dominant class. This aggression does not always present itself in a glaring manner—the cities seem peaceful and the citizens display joyful and satisfied faces. But the misery is becomingly hidden; and not only misery, but also the importance of large sectors of society who cannot step beyond the limits of their restricted social, cultural and economic possibilities. In this case we may well speak of a violence perpetrated by the dominant class, which thus becomes a permanent aggressor against the majority of the citizens. We are therefore faced by the precise case described by classical morality; the victims of aggression have the

86

right to repel this aggression *"servato moderamine inculpatae tuelae,"* seeking to moderate their legitimate self-defence.

Naturally, when we come down to the plane of concrete reality, it will not always be easy to determine the manner in which Christians may dedicate themselves to this struggle. But there can be no doubt as regards the essential fact that, by way of principle, Christians not only have the right but even the duty to take their place in the legitimate struggle of the proletariat for creating a society where the existence of a permanent unjust aggressor shall no longer be possible. When Christians meet together "in order to eat the supper of the Lord," they are not to engage in politics in the technical sense of the word, although they must make a rigorous examination of their collective conscience regarding their duty to dedicate themselves to every creative and humanizing movement.

The Vatican II Council clearly encourages us in this sense.

Every day there is a growing number of men and women, in all groups and in all nations, who are conscious of being the promoters of the culture of their own community. The sense of autonomy, and, at the same time, the sense of responsibility, are continually growing all over the world; this is of enormous importance inasmuch as it favors the spiritual and moral maturity of the human family. This becomes even clearer if we take a look at the unification of the world and the task we have been set of building a better world in truth and in justice. In this way we are witnesses to the fact that a new humanism is being born, in which man is principally defined in terms of his responsibility towards his brothers and towards history.[12]

Now this is an excellent watchword—the Christian's responsibility towards his brothers and towards history. Christians do not have special glands that are different from those of other people and capable of secreting predetermined historical situations. We are only witnesses of a reality that is being born in front of our eyes, and we are the disciples of this reality just like the rest of mankind. A Christian humanism does not exist; but there exist Christians who, even in the name of their faith, dedicate themselves to the constant and growing process of universal humanization.

If, therefore, in the course of this process of humanization there presents itself the pressing need of an unavoidable struggle, the Christian knows that the "parallel" of humanization runs through the interests of the oppressed rather than through the profit of the oppressors. Naturally, the presence of Christians in this possible class struggle will bring with it the conditioning peculiar to the evangelical morality. But we must recognize this evangelical morality is not something preestablished, but rather a very strong impetus towards inventing new attitudes in the face of that unforeseeable reality that in the Bible is referred to as "neighbor."

We do not know who our neighbor is, he is always somebody unknown; and the attitude of the faithful in the face of his neighbor represents a pure choice. We cannot choose our neighbors in advance, and we cannot permit ourselves the luxury of preferring "our more interesting neighbors." In a certain sense our neighbor is a transcendental reality that bursts into our lives and forces us continually to invent our moral attitudes anew.

We Christians participate in this struggle full of love, of hope, and also of anguish. We shall have to experiment, make mistakes, and rectify them. We are not infallible men, but rather seekers of love even in the most difficult situations. In all this we must create a morality and a mystique of revolution, but we must not flee from the battlefield—the battlefield that is about to decide the future of an exploited humanity that is trying to create new structures where exploitation shall no longer be institutionalized.

OVERCOMING A MORAL ALTERNATIVE

But before we can arrive at this point we must first overcome a false moral alternative. Marxists frequently reproach Christians for having a morality of the individual, which does no more than present an isolated and egoistic perspective; they consider the salvation of the soul as an evasion of the immediate tasks that concern man as the creator both of himself and his own history.

Christians, on the other hand, reproach Marxists for considering man as nothing more than a pawn of the grandiose dialectical mechanism that is composed of laws independent of the little problems that assail the individual.

In recent times both Marxists and Christians, in a process in which we are reestablishing our links with our principles and our origins, have begun to reexamine this rigid alternative and quite rightly to insert some dialectical motives into it.

The Polish Marxist philosopher Adam Schaff makes some precise assertions in this respect. In the first place he honestly recognizes that in the contemporary exposition of Marxism there exists a gap that has to be filled. He writes:

Only sociology and social psychology can explain the reasons why a philosopher is today being continually requested, and particularly in meetings of young people, to give answers to questions concerning the meaning of life. I confess that the frequency and the persistence of the question have caused me to reflect and even to change my attitude in the face of this problem.[13]

And he immediately recognizes that Marxist morality is in need of "a more complete picture of the world." Schaff continues:

Marxism teaches that the problem of the individual must be resolved only in a wider social context and that the knowledge of the laws that govern social life is an indispensable condition for properly understanding this problem and resolving it. But Marxism has never asserted that knowledge of the laws of social development exhausts the problems of the individual. For as long as men will continue to die and to be afraid of death, for as long as they will continue to lose their dear ones and to be afraid of losing them, for as long as they will suffer physically and morally—and in one form or other this will happen throughout the duration of the human kind—they will want to know, apart from the laws that govern the successive changes of social formation, how they are to understand their personal problems and how they are to comport themselves. Every theory that aspires to constructing a particular vision of the world must give an answer to these questions, which contribute in a decisive manner to this selfsame conception of the world.[14]

For our own part, we Christians willingly recognize that we have often forgotten the social and historical content within which the life of man is fatefully bound to take its course. And this explains why, in the name of a so-called Christian mystique, we have been absent from the truly revolutionary movements. These, in fact, are concerned with changing the structures; we, however, were too much concerned with changing the individual.

This absence from the revolutionary movements could possibly provide the justification for the fact that the revolutionaries, more concerned with changing the structures, have neglected the individual. In view of the fact that the Christian counterrevolutionaries have excessively emphasized this morality of the individual, the revolutionaries were forced to consider all attention to personal problems as being contrary to the revolution itself.

And this is also the concrete aspect of our contribution to a serious revolutionary impetus—to insert this mystique of the person into the social and historical context of the dynamics of human rise and development.

Conclusions

We have seen that we Christians have concrete and important tasks in the construction of a world that is now being born and is orientating itself towards a socialist solution. In this construction of socialism we Christians do not have a concrete technical solution. The experience of two thousand years teaches us that the *civitas humana* must not be absorbed by the Church; the Church does not have the task of creating its own *civitas* where the Gospels become an economic, political and social code. The *civitas* must construct itself with its own autonomous means. And in view of the fact that throughout the centuries the Church has made the mistake of successively constructing a "feudal Christianity," a "bourgeoise Christianity" and a "democratic Christianity," it must now be careful not to construct a "socialist Christianity." At the very beginning Christianity represented a "secularization" of religion, Jewish as much as Greek. Successively the Church became resacralized, turning its message and its norms into a complete and specific code that completely regulates the life of man.

In very few words, this means that the attitude of the Christian who finds himself in the midst of the *civitas* must constantly maintain itself in a dialectical equilibrium, and overcome the ready temptation to establish oneself in one of the two possible alternatives. There is an alternative of the right—to establish oneself in the counterrevolution, seeking in the Christian message valid motives for condemning the revolutionary movement.

There is also an alternative of the left—seeking in the same message technical solutions in order to carry forward the revolution, or rather to render ineffective the action of the others who have so far been the pioneers.

The two alternatives break up the dialectical equilibrium of the authentic Christian faith. The Christian must play his part in the socialist revolution without bringing with him any technical prejudices, that is to say without becoming arrogantly overbearing in his quality as a believer, and at the same time giving the notable contribution of his mystique of universal brotherhood and total hope.

Because—and we have to recognize this—socialism will never be constructed by the mere blind faith of a mechanically conceived history. Socialism is a free choice of the creative will of man. And the Gospels have always been, and will always continue to be, an immensely effective driving force for putting this free choice into practice.

Chapter Six The Christian Faith and Marxism in Revolution

Paul Blanquart

My aim is a very limited one, but concerns a specific problem: the relationship between Marxism and the Christian faith for those who participate in a revolutionary process. I take my position as a philosopher to propose an intellectual "unblocking" and thereby to promote action by the Christian community. In this sense, what I am about to do might be described as a labor of Christian "intelligence."

THE INEVITABLE CONFRONTATION WITH REVOLUTION AND MARXISM

I want to begin by stressing two things. For the purposes of a political action, I agree with the distinction that has been drawn between the diagnosis and analysis made in order to provide a basis for one's personal choices and the values with which such choices are concerned; this produces a certain existential tension for Christians between the political project thus determined and the evangelical requirements. Each political project thus comprises two components: a rationality that acts in the diagnosis, and a utopia in accordance with the point of view of a believer, the desire for a horizon "inhabited" by the revelation he has received in Jesus Christ of the dimensions of his existence and his future, a horizon that takes the concrete form of a series of values that intervene in the determination of his political choice.

Moreover, I would like to stress that two factors are inevitably required for making a revolution: revolutionary forces and a theory, i.e., a body of concepts that permits these revolutionary forces to act in an effective manner. Just like the previous distinction, this too is primarily a structural one, because the forces and the theory will in practice continuously generate each other in the course of a concrete revolutionary process.

Each revolutionary, be he a Christian or otherwise, will find himself face to face with Marxism, either in the form of a theory or in the form of revolutionary forces.

As a theory Marxism puts forward in a particular manner the analysis of imperialism made by Lenin, together with the necessary extensions, elaborations and corrections required by social evolution; for example, today one notes that the movement of capital has changed direction with respect to the times of Victorian England: it no longer flows from the evolved capitalist countries towards the poor countries, but rather in the opposite direction, and this is in large part due to the integration that is caused by the dominant economic pole, particularly by North American imperialism, and by the present technological and scientific upheaval.

But one finds oneself face to face with Marxism also as an array of forces; these are the forces of the socialist camp, whose solidarity, in spite of all divergencies, is absolutely essential if a revolutionary project is to be successful.

This inevitable confrontation of the revolutionary with Marxism is by itself sufficient, so at least it seems to me, to demonstrate the inadequacy of any project for a "third road" toward which a goodly number of Christians is tending spontaneously and idealistically, just as is done by a goodly number of Christian organizations, but undoubtedly with less idealism. This seems to be a project incapable of mobilizing sufficient forces; on the other hand, any policy of help and assistance that does not take into account the social relationships that are the origin of the injustices and the difficulties of our time is condemned to failure from the outset.

I therefore find myself faced with a problem that I imagine must also be the problem of many other people: what position shall I assume in the inevitable confrontation with Marxism? I should like to make at least some hypotheses and suggestions on the basis of the distinction I recalled at the beginning, the distinction between scientific rationality on the one hand, and on the other, the utopia and the values to which the choices are referred; these latter I would provisionally and rather indistinctly call "ideology."

MARXISM AND CHRISTIAN FAITH: IDEOLOGY AND UTOPIA

What do Marxism and the Christian faith offer me respectively for the purpose of animating and directing political action or, more particularly, revolutionary action?

Marxism offers me three things. First of all a rationality, i.e., an operational model that gives me the possibility of coming to grips with this daily more obvious phenomenon of the growing disparity between opulent and proletarian countries; it offers me an explanation of the causes and suggests some orientations for the solution.

It further offers me an ideology; but this, in turn, presents itself in two forms and, contrary to the usual practice, it is important to distinguish between them. In the first place it presents itself in the form of a revolutionary utopia, the mobilizer of energies: the "total" man of the young Marx, the "integral" man of Cuba, etc. From this point of view there is no rivalry for the faith, because the optics of observation do not concern the question of God and we are dealing with a humanism. But there is a second form of the ideology, i.e., the form of an atheist ideology, and this is the form that causes us difficulty. I use the term ideology in the technically valid sense of the word: a system of representation by means of which or within which man perceives and expresses his overall relationship with the world and with others, and within which he therefore lives the exercise of his rationality and his utopia. This ideology thus poses the principle that revolutionary humanism supposes and contains the negation of God and of the possibility related to us by the revelation that there may be something in common between God and men.

For its own part, what does the Christian faith offer me?

Unlike Marxism, it only offers me two things: a utopia and an ideology.

It is a utopia that contains a considerable evolutionary force, a humanism that is within the fact of the faith and which constitutes a spiritual force that is marvelously capable of offering dynamic forces for a revolution.

The Christian faith also offers me an ideology into which this humanism is poured and which is opposed to atheism inasmuch as it reserves to God a central place in the world and in man. It therefore lacks the third element that Marxism offers me; the Christian faith does not offer me a rationality, i.e., an operational model, a technical analysis of social reality.

I would like to deduce a conclusion from this comparison. First of all, there is no problem between the faith and Marxism on the level of the rationality, i.e., on the level of the operational model elaborated by Marx and particularly transposed onto a world scale by Lenin; moreover, there exists a certain moral convergence on the level of the utopias, of the humanisms: both are in favor of man being fully man; lastly, one must note an opposition at the level of what I have called ideologies: on the one side there is a believing ideology, on the other there is an atheist ideology.

I would now like to clarify some aspects of the distinction between these three levels, and point out a possible fecundity that derives from this distinction. To this end I think it may be useful to quote a text that I prepared and signed together with three priests at the Havana Cultural Congress in January 1968. One of the positions we assumed was the following:

We are convinced, in spite of the differences that exist between Christianity and Marxism as regards the interpretation of man and the world (this is what I have called ideology), that Marxism offers us the most exact scientific analysis of imperialist reality (the level of rationality) and that it offers the most effective stimulus for the revolutionary action of the masses (the level of humanism, the revolutionary utopia).

Later we tried to express the synthesis of these three elements acceptable to a Christian: "We are convinced that the Christian

95

faith (ideology) implies a love (humanism) placed in the effective service (which supposes rationality) of each and every man."

We must certainly admit that this attitude calls in effect for a dissociation of what according to Marx and the greater part of Marxists seemed and still seems to be intrinsically linked: scientific socialism and atheist humanism. This position of ours would therefore introduce a profound revision of the initial unitarianism of Marxist thought.

The problem that we posed ourselves at the beginning therefore assumes a new form: is the Marxist partner disposed to follow us onto the ground I have proposed? This question is extremely important, because what is at stake here is the taking of power, the complete availability of the structures of the state. If the men whom we could help to take power were not to recognize this dissociation, they would immediately translate the revolutionary effort into an antireligious struggle. This is something that has already extensively happened and could easily happen again.

Let us make it quite clear that this is not a question of the atheist ceasing to be an atheist, but simply a question of his stopping to think that the link between atheism, socialism and revolution is absolutely necessary for everybody; it is clear that the absolute assertion of such a link would in practice inevitably reduce the believer, even if he be a citizen and a militant, to a second-class status.

It is true that at Havana we had a favorable reaction from Fidel Castro towards the text we presented and from which I have quoted two passages; he used the text extensively and commented on it at length. But one could think that this reaction was only dictated by a tactical interest (there are many Christians in Latin America and you must have them with you if you want to make a revolution); or that it is only due to the ideological openness that characterizes the Cuban Revolution; or, more simply that one could see in it a reminiscence of the early education received by Fidel Castro.

CAN MARXIST SCIENCE AND IDEOLOGY BE DISSOCIATED?

Faced with this perplexity, and for the purpose of resuming the dialogue with the Marxist partner, I would like to submit the following thesis for discussion and further reflection: Marxism has the greatest interest in effecting this dissociation, and this not only for momentary tactical reasons, but to favor the revolution and its future. This may seem a paradox, but I think that to press for this dissociation is an eminent service that we can render to Marxism, and therefore to the revolution.

First of all, it seems to me that the identification between the operational model and a particular ideology (a true "blockage") lies at the basis of the failures that have manifested themselves in political undertakings on a Marxist foundation; in fact, it led to ignorance of the specificity of the political order. This ignorance disarmed Marxism when faced with the Stalinist dictatorship, with certain phenomena of bureaucratization, and left the field clear for an official ideology to oppress the cultural and spiritual dimension of human existence. This ignorance of the specificity of the political has disarmed Marxism with respect to everything that comes from democracy, and this has been Marxism's greatest stumbling block. It is not a simple coincidence that the great present-day movements in the East are not directed against socialism, but in favor of democracy, and that they are to a large extent the work of students and intellectuals, i.e., of persons whose profession is culture.

The truth is that the claim for cultural liberation is identical with the claim for political democracy and, more particularly, raises the problem of the relationship between the party and an ideology and also between the state and the party, at least to the extent to which the party identifies itself with that ideology (in this case, the ideology of atheist humanism).

As against this, it seems that the dissociation I have proposed gives added value to this necessary specificity of the political. One must, in fact, dissociate the level of ideologies, which can be competitive and opposed, and the scientific level of the operational model in order to be able to comprehend what joins the one to the other, what mediatizes them, i.e., the practical policy that one gives to the specific organisms and institutions, which are neither those of the ideologies nor those of the research laboratories.

It seems that the political area must be understood as the place where different or even opposed ideologies converge and debate (and this is democracy) to establish a common political project within the framework of the organisms and institutions that are popular to the political order; naturally, all this can happen while account is being taken of the data of analyses that are as scientific as possible (let us do everything we can in the field of the so-called human sciences) and the results of scientific rationality.

In this perspective I must confess that I cannot understand the position of those who refuse Marxism purely and simply in order to save some ideological, cultural or religious originality. People talk about an "African socialism" which, in order to be such must keep its due distance from Marxism. I don't know whether this is the best way of posing the problem; I am also asking myself whether putting the problem in this way is not at the origin of the fact that this "socialism," which is greatly talked about in the leading circles of some countries, is in practice anything but socialism.

Numerous representatives of the Third World at the Havana Cultural Congress vigorously stressed the need for ensuring the vitality of the cultural peculiarities of the various peoples and the various civilizations if one wants the revolution to be the real revolution, i.e., a liberation of man. But this assertion of cultural specificities did not by any means seem to call into question their adherence to a common operational model, the model of Marxist socialism; moreover, this adherence seems to be all the more necessary because, faced by a system of world domination, one has to put into practice a worldwide revolutionary strategy.

On this level we can expect a great deal from what one might call the "Marxism of the three continents," which regards national emancipation as one and the same thing as the socialist project.

At this point there is a very obvious objection: all this would be very well, but how can one ask the impossible of Marxists? I do not think that one is asking the impossible, because it seems to me that the evolution of Marxist thought is itself going in this direction, almost irresistibly so, under the pressure of the facts.

The principal problem that is presently posing itself with growing acuteness in the countries of the East is the moral problem, the problem of humanism. The contribution made by a Czechoslovak philosopher during a "Week of Marxist Thought" recently held at Paris is rather interesting. Among other things he said this: What we need more than anything else in Czechoslovakia is faith. He then added: "A faith without God," and he evidently did this in order not to create difficulties for an assembly that was beginning to ask itself questions at this point; he went on to say that this was a case of a faith in man that was objectively required by the new productive conditions; the state of poverty has now been left behind; it is no longer a case of producing more, but rather producing better (a need for "optimization" rather than "maximization"), and this introduces criteria peculiar to the order of subjectivity and not amenable to the calculation of economic rationality. On the other hand, the technological upheaval puts a premium on the creative aspects of human intelligence. In the Marxist countries, therefore, they visualize the possibilities of a faith to enable the revolution to continue.

We now know the vigorous reaction of the Althusser school with respect to this need of humanism, and this seems to me to be fecund with perspectives because it defines the data of the problem more clearly; in fact, it puts us on our guard by recalling a particular fact: Marxism is primarily a science, and for this very reason is not a humanism. In order to revalue these scientific claims of Marxism, it draws a very clear distinction between the level of the science or the theory and the field of ideology. The distinction is so sharp that for the Althusser school there is no relationship between these two fields. One has to cross a very deep ditch, which is called an "epistemological break," in order to arrive at the banks of science, to be able to create theories. In other words, ideology has no place in science, something that the specialists in the exact sciences have realized for a long time.

The outcome of the evolution that I would personally consider to be desirable seems to me to be clearly indicated in a statement made by Josef Hindels, an Austrian Marxist in reply to a question about Marxist atheism. Inasmuch as Marxism has something specific to give to our times, he said, it considers itself as a science and is not therefore concerned with taking up a position for or against God.

How Can Integrationism and Dogmatism Be Overcome?

I think that if we want to find a solution to the problem of the relationship between Marxism and Christian faith, we must endeavor to accelerate this evolution of the traditional Marxists. But how can this be done in a concrete way? I do not think that this can be done through debates among philosophers alone, but will be primarily achieved in the course of action itself.

On the one hand they should understand that we can be socialists and anti-imperialists just like themselves, that we can be just as hard-headed as they when it comes to the needs of rationality, that we can participate in the theoretical work of developing and refining the operational model, and that we can therefore come completely onto their ground and yet remain believers.

We can convince them, always in the concrete course of action and the revolutionary process, of the possibility of their evolution, showing them that our Christian specificity can bring particular riches to the revolution itself, and can contribute to the enrichment of the utopia.

Concrete work in this direction may lead the Marxists, who are as yet too often dogmatic and integralist in this sector, to understand that they have every interest in effecting the dissociation of which I have spoken. And when they will have understood their interest, discussion will become possible at the level of political institutions and organizations, just as it will become possible at this level to recognize the plurality of ideologies, and therefore democracy.

This would make it possible in future to avoid the results of the "blockage" that is still too often operated by Marxist leaders and intellectuals; it is sterile and unbecoming for Christians and I have already denounced it; but it is a "blockage" that history is increasingly showing to be—and during the last few months this has been particularly evident in the East European countries—just as sterile and destructive for socialism itself.

Chapter Seven Search for a Phenomenology of Revolution

P. L. Geschiere and H. G. Schulte Nordholt

INTRODUCTION

Revolution is a burning problem—whoever concerns himself with it is apt to burn his fingers. This applies equally to the churches and to scientists. Matters are no different in the social sciences. No mention of revolution is even made in the 3,000 columns of the great work entitled *Theories of Society* published in 1962 and edited by leading American sociologists Talcott Parsons, Edward Skills, Kaspar D. Naegele and Jesse R. Pitts.

Revolution in the sense in which we use it is only a relatively new concept. It was originally an astronomical term (Copernicus, for example, wrote *"De revolutionibus orbium coelestium"*) used with reference to the revolutions made by celestial bodies. The word was borrowed in that sense by authors on history and politics. In England the word was first used when the Stuarts returned in 1660. Cromwell's rebellion was not a revolution, but the restoration of the monarchy under William and Mary was the definitive reestablishment of the ancient legal order, termed the "Glorious Revolution." The word revolution in its modern sense was probably used for the first time when the Bastille fell on July 14, 1789, when Louis XVI said:

"C'est un revolte!" and his gentleman-in-waiting replied "Non, sire, c'est une révolution!"

This marked the beginning of the development of the entire complex of concepts known as the French Revolution. The world can change radically and man is capable of effecting this new order. The desire for a total change, for a golden age or paradise lost, is felt in many cultures, especially in times of distress. And all peoples which have been brought into contact with Judeo-Christian Messianism are familiar with the quest for the millennium; and they are not alone in this.

These notions are inherent in all present-day revolutionary movements, the one great difference being that it is not the return to an earlier condition, or a rebirth or renaissance, no return *ad fontes* as in the Reformation, not a profound and total rejection of the present evil world as in all millenarianism, that is desired. What is wanted is progress.

Condorcet in his *Esquisse d'un Tableau Historique des Progres de l'Esprit Humain* (1793) professes his belief in a perfect future man. Comte developed this further in his "positivistic" concepts of development and progress.

But after Darwin's time this notion of progress came to be linked with the concept of evolution of the natural sciences. Then the notion that revolution is inevitable acquired the added connotation that it is not only a historical necessity but that its course itself is as unchangeable as that of the stars. This brings us back to Copernicus. And it shows up a contradiction in terms. In the statements of most revolutionaries, their aim was to create a new world, whereas those who had revolted, who had been through the school of revolutionism, knew beforehand what the inevitable course must be. They knew the French Revolution was exceedingly violent and so they wanted violence. They knew that revolution devours its own children and yet they fought for freedom. Thus they became "the fools of history," to quote Hannah Arendt.

This hardly explains why the social sciences have given so little of their attention to the phenomenon of revolution. It is important enough. *The New York Times* alone reported well over 1,200 unequivocal examples between 1946 and 1959 (civil wars, including guerrilla wars, localized rioting, widely dispersed turmoil, organized and apparently unorganized terrorism, mutinies, and coups d'etat). Only a handful of societies have managed to remain highly tranquil in the general commotion (Eckstein).

But even this handful of societies has known war and tremendous tensions. It is especially a result of these very circumstances that sociologists began to look for organic solidarity (Durkheim), integration and equilibrium. Words such as deviance, discontinuity and conflict, on the other hand, are negatively loaded. Crane Brinton in his book, *The Anatomy of Revolution*, still describes revolution in terms of pathology. It is only recently that people have begun to realize that social conflict and social change, and even social development are highly correlated. However, social change is a change which takes place in the course of time; it is a historical process. The social sciences are not well equipped theoretically for historical research.

Ever since these sciences quite rightly turned away from the pseudo-history of the old evolutionary school and from diffusionism, they have concentrated on synchronic reality, using empiric methods, with social environment techniques like social-survey analysis, experimentation in controlled situations, and field work. This makes it difficult to catch social change in the act, and revolutions put even greater difficulties in the way of interviewers, fieldworkers and pollsters. There is no equivalence between the tools and the material. Social theorists confronted by the subject are understandably at sea—like shoemakers working not on leather but on ox, says Eckstein.

History has always concerned itself with conflict, war and revolution. Until quite recently it was at a loss as to how to deal with peace. The solution of these problems can only be found if historic science is prepared to cooperate with the other social sciences, and these in turn are prepared to learn from its methods how to be able to say more about the problems of revolution as a general phenomenon. For we are living in a revolutionary age, and the developing countries are showing a great deal of interest in Marxism. They are struggling with slowly progressing processes of modernization. Their economic development is slowest of all. If they could resort to revolution, the superstructure, according to Marxism, would automatically follow the infrastructure which determines it. There is a general revolutionary élan not only in the developing countries but in the developed countries as well. Their aims are usually rather ill defined but they are mostly potentially inclined towards violence.

A Definition of Revolution

The definition of the phenomenon of revolution poses great difficulties.

As a result of the French Revolution the term acquired the restricted, unequivocal meaning of a sudden, violent upheaval in political and social structures. In jurisprudence and political science it is sometimes still restricted to a juridical definition as well as that made by political science such as: "the seizure of the state power—usually by violent means—by a person or grouping which introduces drastic changes in a particular political structure." This even leaves room for the possibility of a nonviolent coup d'etat. Johnson, in his book *Revolution and the Social System* takes Neumann's definition as his point of departure, viz.: revolution is "a sweeping, fundamental change in political organization, social structure, economic property control and the predominant myth of a social order, thus indicating a major break in the continuity of development." Generally speaking the concept of revolution has gradually expanded, partly under the influence of socio-economic historiography which began to use the term "industrial revolution." In the social sciences revolution came to be defined as "a sudden and far reaching major break in the continuity of development" (*Dictionary of Social Sciences*, 1933). This meaning has been adopted by general usage. The term gradually became more and more vague.

The vital question, namely what exactly is to be understood by revolution, remains unanswered. It is not for the social sciences to force a particular definition of "revolution" upon general usage. If sociology were to manipulate its own, more limited definitions, the result would be a confusion of tongues. New terms are therefore being sought, such as the term "Internal War" which has been borrowed to serve as a title for the bundle of essays edited by Eckstein. The objection against this term is that it does not express the aim toward drastic structural changes

105

in society. It is desirable not to deviate too much in scientific terminology from the definition of revolution as "a sudden and far reaching major break," in other words, far reaching structural changes in many aspects of culture. When using the term revolution it is necessary to specify further whether revolution implies violence or whether a nonviolent revolution is meant, in order to avoid the risk of being vague and of applying the epithet revolutionary to oneself without being revolutionary in the eyes of others.

SOME IMPORTANT CHARACTERISTICS OF THE PHENOMENON OF REVOLUTION

We should not merely give a definition of the phenomenon of revolution, but—what is more important still—endeavor to point out a few of its important elements. Some of these elements follow:

1. *The desire for renewal.* Not all characteristics of revolution are present in every case. An indication of certain basic characteristics of revolution will help us arrive at some models of a revolution while the presence of some characteristics and the absence of others will make a typology possible.

The most fundamental characteristic of a revolution is the desire for change and belief in the possibility of effecting change. All revolutionaries have had visions of the beginning of a new era. Only where this pathos of novelty is present are we entitled to speak of revolution. This renewal is concentrated on the political, social, and economic structures seen as a totality. The "pathos of novelty" is possible only if backed by a myth of a new social order or of a new world which can only be realized through a sudden break with the existing order.

2. *Liberation and liberty.* In addition to this, and intimately bound up with it, we have the notion of liberty which marks every revolution. Liberty and liberation should be clearly distinguished here. In every revolution there is a consciousness of an unbearable yoke which must be thrown off. The liberation from tyranny or from foreign dominance is prerequisite for attaining liberty, that is, if the revolution is a political one; if it is a social

revolution, it is necessary to liberate oneself from a position of social inferiority and from economic exploitation.

Therefore liberty is a negative condition in the initial phase, as it involves liberating oneself from a certain condition. The next problem is the realization of liberty. It is here that the tragedy of most revolutions is most poignant, for in spite of the fight for freedom, freedom is not achieved. This is the problem to which Hannah Arendt devotes the greater part of her book, *On Revolution.*

She contrasts the American Revolution with the French Revolution, and in a most penetrating analysis arrives at the conclusion that the American Revolution was successful in achieving freedom as it was a political revolution. Not because there were no social problems—400,000 people lived in bondage and only as a result of their toil were the other 1,850,000 people (Europeans) who lived in the United States about the middle of the eighteenth century able to live free from poverty—but because these social problems were simply overlooked, as they were by the French who personally witnessed the struggle for freedom in America and were inspired by it. After liberation it was possible to provide for the liberty of the American citizen in the *constitutio libertatis* by laying down and guaranteeing the citizens' inalienable civil rights and his freedom to participate in public affairs. In France, however, tension arose between the ideal of political freedom and the necessity for solving the social problem. Robespierre's words: *"Je ne connais que la question sociale"* fully expressed this. And this "transformation of the Rights of Man into the rights of Sans-Culottes was the turning point not only of the French Revolution but of all revolutions that were to follow."

3. *The dominant influence of the French Revolution.* Marx as a young man was convinced that the French Revolution failed to found freedom because it had failed to solve the social question. From this he concluded that freedom and poverty were incompatible. And this social question is transformed into a political force in the term "exploitation," in the notion that poverty is the result of exploitation through a "ruling class" which is in the

possession of the means of violence. As a result of the formation of theories during, but especially after the French Revolution, the latter served as a model for all following revolutions, especially the Bolshevik Revolution.

4. *The inevitability of the course of revolution.* This imitation of the French model is primarily the result of the conception of the inevitability of the course of a revolution. The first phase is liberation, followed by dictatorship; the revolution must inevitably devour its own children in a series of successive revolutions. There are suspects who must be unmasked, and there come into being two factions—the *indulgents* and the *enragés*—which actually work together in order to undermine the revolutionary government.

Then the revolution is saved by the man in the middle, who, far from being moderate, liquidates the right and the left as Robespierre had liquidated Danton and Heber.

> The magic spell which historical necessity has cast over the minds of men since the beginning of the nineteenth century has had the same profound meaningfulness of first crystallizing the best of men's hopes and then realizing the full measure of their despair that the French Revolution had for its contemporaries (Hannah Arendt).

This theory of the inevitability of the tide of revolution still finds firm belief among revolutionaries such as Fidel Castro. It is this notion that has not only constituted an important characteristic of revolution since 1789, but even encourages the revolutionary situation and influences the course of a revolution.

5. *Human goodness and pity.* Christianity has always taught—albeit in various gradations—that man is sinful. The French Revolution, thinking along the lines of Locke and Rousseau, presupposed that man was good by nature. This goodness found its highest expression in the pity for *le peuple toujours malheureux*, as Sieyes, down to earth as he was, put it. For the revolutionaries this pity for the people, for the masses in their infinite vulgarity was the greatest, most exalted virtue.

But pity, taken as the spring of virtue, has proved to possess a greater capacity for cruelty than cruelty itself. *"Pas pitié, pas amour pour l'humanité, soyez inhumans!"* are the words in a petition to the National Convention in Paris. "These words are neither accidental nor extreme; they are the authentic language of pity," says Hannah Arendt. She refers in this connection to Herman Melville's great short story *Billy Budd, Foretopman,* written during the last years of his life. The problem brought forward in his story is that the end of the eighteenth century "involved a crisis for Christendom" as never before, and that the French Revolution "involved rectification of the Old World's hereditary wrongs." "In France this was bloodily effected. But what then? Straightway the Revolution itself became a wrongdoer." (Preface, Belgrade ed., 1966). Billy Budd is representative of primitive man who is endowed with "barbaric" innocence. The topic of the story is goodness beyond virtue and evil beyond vice. Goodness, because it is part of "nature," does not act weakly, but asserts itself forcefully and indeed violently so that we are convinced: only the violent act with which Billy Budd strikes dead the man who bore false witness against him is adequate; it eliminates nature's "depravity."

Thus begins the story. Virtue, in the person of Captain Vere, is introduced into the conflict between absolute good and absolute evil. The false witness was "struck by an angel of God, yet the angel must hang." Hannah Arendt says with reference to this:

Clearly, Melville reversed the primordial legendary crime, Cain slew Abel, which has played such an enormous role in our tradition of political thought, but this reversal is not arbitrary; it followed from the reversal the men of the French Revolution had made of the proposition of original sin, which they had replaced by the proposition of original goodness. —Let us suppose that from now on the foundation stone of our political life will be that Abel slew Cain. Don't you see that from this deed of violence the same chain of wrongdoing will follow, only that now mankind will not even have the consolation that the violence it must call crime is indeed characteristic of evil men only?

In the present-day revolutionary situation this problem is as topical as at the time of the French Revolution.

6. *A general feeling of discomfort.* In every revolution the masses can only be stirred into activity if there is a feeling of se-

rious discomfort, which is generally connected with drastic changes, such as a lost war, a tyranny which is becoming constantly more insupportable, a breakdown of the economy or other changes essentially affecting the life of the masses. Poverty by itself is not a characteristic of revolution. People have suffered poverty throughout the history of mankind, and only the thought that change and renewal are possible makes poverty and political abuses insupportable. What is more, in the developing countries themselves the contrasts between a small wealthy and privileged elite and the large mass of paupers are becoming more pronounced. In the colonial period the elite consisted chiefly of strangers, whereas at present it is, as in Latin America, an autochthonous elite. Moreover, these contrasts are becoming more obvious and more poignant, as the elite is able to indulge in the luxury of the modern technical culture of the West.

7. *Representation of the masses.* The masses themselves, especially if very poor, are not easily aroused to action. A general lethargy is a frequent characteristic of rural societies leading a marginal existence. Leaders who are able to give the necessary inspiration for renewal are required. The words *le peuple* are the key words for every understanding of the French Revolution. But these masses, this proletariat, lacks the opportunity of giving its consent by means of representation to the intentions and aims of the leaders. In the French Revolution the hierarchy of the monarchy was eliminated, but freedom from tyranny actually meant freedom for a few. The people continued to be weighed down by the burden of its misery. Then, when the social revolution began its course, Robespierre postulated emphatically that "the laws should be promulgated in the name of the French people instead of the French Republic." It could not but follow from this—speaking in retrospect—that almost as a matter of course Rousseau's *volonté generale* should replace the ancient notion of consent which, in Rousseau's theory, may be found as the *volonté de tous.* "Consent," with its overtones of deliberate choice and considered opinion, was replaced by the word "will," which essentially excludes all processes of exchange of opinions. The will, if it is to function at all, must indeed be one and indivisible.

110

Robespierre demanded: "Il faut une volonté unie." This will finds expression in and through the leaders. This has remained a central idea in all revolutionary movements up to the present day and it is the reason (possibly even the excuse) for revolutionary governments omitting to ask the peoples' consent for their political actions and for their refusal to admit freedom of speech and consequently the expression of a variety of opinions.

8. *Revolutionaries have no eye for variations in the situation.* The men of the French Revolution improvised most of their actions on the spur of the moment. Each revolution has its own, unique course. Placing different revolutions side by side with each other, as historians are apt to do in historical compilations, is misleading, therefore scientists can derive but few general rules from this. However, this is not so with the disposition of revolutionaries. We have already noted how they have always looked up to the French Revolution as an example and in doing so believed in the inevitability of the course of the revolution. In addition to this they have overlooked the wide cultural differences in the large number of countries which they now consider ripe for revolution. The situation is constantly viewed in terms borrowed from the Western "capitalistic" world. The question is whether the masses in the Third World are comparable to the proletariat of nineteenth-century Europe. We should furthermore refer in this connection to the observations concerning nation building; a central institutional framework for channelling the activities of the masses is still absent.

Partly as a result of this circumstance the opinions of the masses are often extremely difficult to assess, and the masses themselves are even more difficult to stir into activity and to control. However that may be, the point of departure of every revolution is determined by the culture of the country in question (culture is here used in the broader sense of the totality of all aspects of life). If that is so, its progress and results will also be dependent on the culture. It is obvious once more that a closer cooperation between historians and social scientists is needed. Cultural anthropologists are able to form an important connecting link in this respect by using the structural-historical method in their approach.

9. *The belief in the manipulability of society.* The view that man is capable of creating his society and his culture in accordance with his own design of the blueprint he has made of it is closely connected with the above. Culture is undeniably man-made, though not artificially by scientists or in the revolutionary struggle.

In the first place the difference in point of departure in every single case, i.e. the differences in the cultures which it is intended to change should be taken into account. In a history of many centuries each and every one of the many cultures has developed its own structures. And it is on the rugged rock formations of these historically developed structures that the new must be built. This involves that planning will have to be different in every case. But apart from that the opportunities for transformation through revolution or any other means are limited, in the first place because the network of structures of a culture is so complicated, and so much the field of different branches of science, that an overall picture of and insight into the various ways of acting and the results of human interference must needs fall short.

Moreover, instead of one single design for transformation, there are numerous designs, which are regarded as political objectives by a large number of powers. This is true on a national level, but especially so on an international one. Culture is the creation of man, but it requires control and power. Power is needed when social and economic changes are to be made. And history shows us that man is only too often powerless to realize his ideals and objectives.

10. *Impatience.* Every revolution is characterized by intense impatience—the new must come and the existing order is intolerable. When we add to this the belief in the manipulability of society as the social sciences view it more or less, this impatience becomes an important characteristic of revolution. Hopes are set high, and the belief that liberation will bring liberty and that social distress will be allayed, is strong. An accurate scien-

tific investigation instituted to discover whether the establishment of freedom and the eradication of poverty have been the direct consequences of any revolution would be essential in this connection.

To what extent do impatience, hope and expectation in a modern revolution essentially differ from these same states in any kind of millenarianism in general? To what extent are utopia and scientific planning for transformation in a revolution distinguishable? Hannah Arendt suggests that the social problem can never be solved by a revolution. In Europe neither the French Revolution nor Marx was able to supply the solution. It has been brought by the progress of technology.

11. *The sense of vocation.* Eugen Rosenstock-Huessey says: "Die Weltrevolutionen von denen die Weltgeschichte allein handeln kann, sind die Umwälzungen, die sich der Welt mitteilen willen." (History can only concern itself with revolutions that want to communicate themselves to the world.)

This utterance tells us more of historical science than of revolution, but it underlines quite clearly the aspect of the sense of vocation inherent in revolution. This does not apply principally to the revolution-makers—it applies partly to them—but much more to revolutionary thinkers. The typical philosophy of revolution, of which paragraphs 4-10 set out a number of aspects, also includes the prophetic urge to spread revolution. These apostles hasten to spread the gospel of liberation. Revolution is in a certain sense a religious belief.

THE SITUATION IN WHICH A REVOLUTION MAY BE SPARKED OFF

Social scientists are not able to say much about the history of revolution, but apply themselves all the more to the analysis of situations which may possibly be ripe for revolution. This is very apparent in the important collection of essays entitled *Internal War* (ed. Harry Eckstein). Nonetheless, in forming a judgment of the situation, they will invariably compare it, consciously or subconsciously, with situations which have actually sparked off a revolution and disprove the models of revolution thus arrived

113

at by comparison with situations in which a revolution had *not* been engendered.

In this context it may be important to supply a few models of revolutionary situations. But we should point out that social scientists who have concerned themselves with revolution have by no means reached agreement on this issue. Revolution is, as we pointed out above, a recent phenomenon. Historians and theoreticians have written volumes on the subject. We know what the course of revolution is, we know the thoughts on revolution of philosophers and revolutionaries, but systematic study of the phenomenon of revolution was only begun for the reasons stated in the introduction. It is by no means surprising that there is as yet a great deal of confusion in this matter. After all the phenomenon is an exceedingly complex one.

There are partial models, in which some of the characteristics mentioned by us are given in relation to each other as well as more comprehensive models. The partial models are open to the danger of biased determinism; apparently it is frequently forgotten that they approach the phenomenon only partially, or their designers sometimes even consciously refuse to regard them as partial models.

1. The classical example of this is Marx's model of revolution. It is worthy of our admiration in that it was the first to discover a fundamental truth; but one-sided in that this discovery did not do full justice to the complexity of reality. Even today Marx's model is important, in the first place because of the degree of truth it contains, and, what is more important, because of the tremendous attraction it holds for many developing countries.

In later life Marx put his views on the structure of society at the basis of his model of revolution. He distinguished society into an infrastructure (production techniques) and a superstructure, the former completely determining the latter. Production techniques, depending on their nature, give rise to different production and ownership relations, which in turn are responsible for the development of social classes. And invariably every effort will be made to maintain the power relations which have

114

developed on the basis of a particular production technique, in spite of changes in production techniques. Changes in production techniques, however, provide for constantly more effective counter-forces, and the struggle between these two opposing forces finally culminates in revolution. Here lies the historical necessity of revolution mentioned previously. The idea that the introduction of raw production techniques alone will bring progress holds much attraction for the developing countries.

2. H. Janne ("Un Modele Theorique du Phenomene Revolutionne?" *Annales,* 1960, II, pp. 1138-54) also takes the structure of society as his point of departure. Revolution according to him is the transition from one structure to another.

a b c d e	
1	1. governing class
2	2. technical and executive frameworks
3	3. lower middle classes
4	4. the masses

a. political organization
b. armed forces
c. churches
d. industry
e. other

Vertical stratification here is provided by the main functional organizations of the society, which are placed side by side, as it were (church, industry, armed forces, political parties, and so on), and each of which repeats the horizontal stratification of the total society. As all vertical organizations share the same culture, namely that of the total society, be it with a different emphasis, they have a strongly integrative influence on the society.

The horizontal stratification consists of the "classical" strata of social hierarchy, characterized by roughly the same mentality, similar interests and a similar way of life. Each of these horizontal strata undergoes the culture of the total society in its own way and constitutes a subculture, and hence lacks an integrative influence.

The above diagram, according to Janne, reproduces the tension inherent in the intersection of horizontal and vertical layers. This is where the phenomenon of revolution has its origin. The top layer represents the culture of the whole, and when a lower layer begins to rebel against it—after a process of awakening consciousness—and is victorious, this subculture in turn will determine the whole. As a result a different structure of society has come about.

In a society with rigid horizontal stratification there is a serious revolutionary potential. Janne does not indicate what conditions are necessary for such a situation to engender revolution. An indication of structures says little concerning the historical process.

3. The third model we wish to mention is that of Ch. Johnson (*Revolution and the Social System,* Stanford Univ., 1964). He bases his work on the old (superseded) view that society is a functionally integrated system containing different structures that are in a state of equilibrium.

However, when internal or external pressure is exerted on the members of a structure, so that they begin to take a different view of their roles, disfunction will be the result. If the action undertaken to counteract this disfunction meets with opposition on the part of the elite this disfunction may spread over several other structures. Thus he arrives at the formula:

multiple disfunction + elite intransigence + x = revolution

x being the factor which sparks off the revolution (x stands for the accelerators of disfunction), the catalyst which brings the process to a critical point. This too is a theoretical model which will have to be brought to life by the multiplicity of historical processes.

4. James C. Davies ("Toward a Theory of Revolution," *Am. Soc. Rev.* 1962, 27, pp. 5-19) subscribes to Marx's theory of *Verelendung,* according to which man resorts to revolution when his conditions grow constantly worse, "because he has nothing to lose but his fetters."

De Tocqueville contradicts this by saying that people are much more apt to resort to revolution after an improvement in their conditions because then they no longer regard poverty as inevitable. Davies accepts the two in combination when he says: "It appears that both ideas have explanatory and possible predictive value if they are juxtaposed and put in proper time sequence." For an inclination towards revolution the constant *expectation* of greater prosperity to satisfy one's wants, on the one hand, and a serious *threat* to the satisfaction of these wants, which has already been partially realized, on the other, are both prerequisites.

This is illustrated by the following diagram:

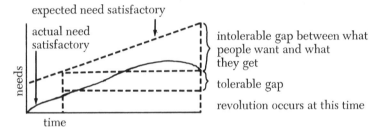

The question remains whether this model can be disproved by referring to the Depression of the thirties, unless it may be assumed that expectation also declined, but in that case the model would hardly serve any purpose. We could also suppose the reverse of this situation to be a revolutionary situation:

These models supply little beyond a theoretical frame of some sort. They set out a few of the necessary conditions for a revolutionary situation but are unable to say whether these conditions are in fact sufficient for a revolution to break out.

117

Ch. Johnson (*Revolution and the Social System*) enumerates various types of revolution.

1. We may leave aside *Jacquerie* (peasant revolt) as it is a rebellion and not a revolution.

2. The *millenarian rebellion* is exceedingly important for the Third World and is typified by a few important characteristics of revolution. It knows "the hope of a complete and radical change in the world which will be reflected in the millennium, a world shorn of its present deficiencies." But the extremely revolutionary philosophy which distinguishes the French Revolution and all modern revolutions is absent here, whereas, on the other hand, the Messianic expectation or *ratu adil* (= just ruler, who played an important part in the Javanese insurrection at the beginning of the nineteenth century) is absent in modern revolution.

3. In addition to this there is the phenomenon of *anarchism.* Johnson is slightly puzzled by it. It was no longer very important after Bakunin, but it is gaining in importance at present. We shall not deal with it because, as far as we can see, it does not play a role in the young states.

4. Finally, there is the *Jacobin-Communist revolution* on which all the important characteristics mentioned above are focused.

5. Johnson mentions the *militarized mass insurrection* as a separate type. It is really a separate, better thought-out and more developed form of the Jacobin-Communist revolution. Examples of militarized mass insurrection (M.M.I.) are: Ireland, 1916-23, Algeria, 1954-62, and so on. But the most important example is China between 1937 and 1948. As early as 1936 Mao Tse-tung postulated the outline of the strategy that was eventually to lead to communist victory in 1949. This strategy may be divided into five main components:

(1) Mobilization of a sustained population. Mass support is the sine qua non of true guerrilla operations. This is categorically

asserted by Mao and continued by Che Guevara (*Guerrilla Warfare 1961*).

(2) Organization of the mobilized population. The final stage of this organization is a "rebel infra structure" or "autonomous government." Maoist theory calls for internal bases. However, it is possible that the bases may exist outside the territorial limits of the target system—i.e. in so called "privileged sanctuaries."

(3) Building of a large revolutionary army on a party member nucleus. The army in a military mass insurrection depends upon the population for the effectiveness of the very military operations themselves. Strict discipline is essential therefore.

(4) Perfection of suitable military tactics. "Guerrilla warfare is the method of fighting in partisan units or with relatively small groups of the regular army disguised as civilians and mingling with the people," as a Chinese author says.

(5) The commitment to a protected war. Guerrilla warfare is the beginning of the end of the revolution, but it is not the end. Finally, when victory is certain, they revert to positional warfare. The battle of Dien Bien Phu is classic in this respect.

In essence militarized mass insurrection strategy is one of developing a mass following *and* of using this mass following to serve a coherent policy. The M.M.I. is a mass revolution under conscious direction from above.

VIOLENCE

What sense is there in using violence if it only achieves liberation and not liberty, and if it does not solve the social problem?

According to Fanon revolution against colonialism will bring about a complete reversal because the use of violence is inevitable here. It even has a positive function. At the level of the masses violence will result in a breakthrough of primordial sentiments; through violence a new nation will be fashioned. "La mobilisation des masses, quand elle se realise a l'occasion de la guerre de liberation, introduit dans chaque conscience la notion de cause commune, de destin national, d'histoire collective." And after the struggle for freedom, violence will offer a valuable contribution to the process of nation-building; it does vary with regionalism and tribalism. This is a practically universal experience in ex-colonies which have had to fight for their freedom. Fanon goes even further and credits violence with an essential role "au niveau des individus." "La Violence debarasse le colonise de son complex d'inferiorité de ses attitudes comtemplatives ou désespérées." This is not rebuked by the post-colonial situation either, although we should point out that generalizations should be handled with care in this connection. Countries which have not had to fight for their freedom are also coping with the problem of overcoming tribalism and in almost all of these the feeling of the inferiority has been conquered without the violence of a war of liberation.

Moreover, no mention is made here of the establishment of freedom or the solution of the social problem. Here, too, Fanon opts for the use of violence. The systematic use of violence for guerrilla strategy in Latin America has been worked out by Che Guevara and Regis Debray. What is aimed at here is the acquisition of political power by means of total and violent revolution following the example of Mao Tse-tung's militarized mass revolution, without clearly defining the ideals for the future or, even worse, selecting the processes of development, as all attention is focused on the immediate objective.

Wertheim's views on violence in a preliminary study for his book *Evolution and Revolution* are more subtle, more cautious, and especially better thought-out. "A revolutionary upsurge of the organized rural proletariat," according to him, is essential in the modernization process. He predicts a fairly strongly determined development in most young states—following more or less the line of thought of the inevitability of the historical process. The starting point of this evolution lies in the rural society. In this context internal conflicts are as yet more or less unpronounced and in the opposition to colonialism and neo-colonialism especially a unitary national ideology develops, in many cases supported to a high degree by a more or less charismatic leader. Wertheim terms this populism; Sukarno and Marhaenism are examples of it.

At present the "efficient administrator" type of leader—i.e. educated specialists, bureaucrats and particularly the army—is constantly gaining more power instead of solidarity-makers like Sukarno. In the existing constellation the bureaucrats and the armed forces will invariably support the status quo, so that class distinctions become even more marked. The entire process will therefore eventually culminate in a (violent) "revolutionary upsurge of the organized rural proletariat," and in many cases this breakthrough in particular will supposedly result in a great leap forward in the modernization process. This final phase could then be the guerrilla strategy of Mao Tse-tung and the Latin American revolutionaries. This overlooks, however, the differences in culture (in China, for example, in Indonesia, Africa and Latin America) mentioned above, as well as the possibility of the bureaucracy and the army becoming important factors in the modernization process (the reader is referred to the first part of this chapter). But most of all, the power and powerlessness of man and the personal qualities of the leader are insufficiently taken into account, as are the external factors.

The question is also whether class distinctions will in fact arise in the Third World. President Nyerere of Tanzania categorically denies this for his country and as far as Indonesia is concerned B. Gunawan's book *Kudeta, Staatsgreep in Indonesie,* 1968 (on the 1964 coup d'etat) is interesting in this context. The latter suggests that in the clash between communists and Muslims plus nationalists there was not so much a question of class distinctions as of a conflict between different currents (*aliran*).

Finally, the question is whether violence is necessary. To begin with we should state that there exists a great deal of violence and that it is used by those in power at present in order to maintain their position. The kind of violence meant should be clearly distinguished however. The reign of the rulers of the ancient African kingdoms was a violent one, but no one disputed the legitimacy of this royal violence. Only in the case of a major part of the population contesting the legitimacy of the leaders, as in the Latin American situation, can we speak of *violencia blanca*. This is very strong and increases in proportion with the increase in opposition. Violence is countered with violence. This thesis is a generally accepted one. Nonetheless it is the duty of scientists to try and disprove theses of this kind. If the *violencia blanca* is overwhelmingly strong and effective there will be no counter-violence, but rather blunt resignation. The experience of colonial dominance does not completely support the thesis.

The superior power of white dominance was overwhelming and it intimidated and in some cases even aroused admiration, especially in Africa. In Indonesia white dominance was on the one hand often considered inevitable and accepted as *insjuh Allah,* the will of Allah, while on the other hand in some areas it met with fierce opposition. The gradual awakening of consciousness as a result of various processes of development was accompanied by doubts about the legitimacy of the oppressor and by his rejection. The question then remains whether violence is the most effective tactic. In South America the situation is even more complex as there *violencia blanca* is exercised by an autochthonous, intransigent elite which prevents processes of development, while the army, the agent of national unity at the beginning of the nineteenth century, is a mere instrument in the hands of a government which is not considered legitimate by the majority. We should here pose the question as to what we can expect to be the results of revolution on the basis of scientific prediction.

1. In the first place it requires the sacrifice of human lives, in accordance with the method of militarized mass insurrection. The major part of the intransigent elite is usually massacred. And the belief that a small number of moderate persons (Christians, for example) can have any influence for the better on this is unrealistic. The pattern of thought in respect of revolution shows us that a process of violence is thought to be inevitable. Up to the present day there have been no deviations from this pattern.
2. As a result revolution will also liquidate the existing influential framework of "capitalistic" enterprises. Hence a new start will

have to be made at an even lower level than what was formerly the lowest.

3. The most serious objection to revolution, however, is that of external influences, which are unavoidable in the factual situation of a modern world which is constantly shrinking, as any revolution, wherever it may take place, becomes a factor in the international politics of the major powers. As a result violence will assume greater proportions and the number of victims increase. Spain and Vietnam are the shocking examples of this. Every new "Vietnam" will involve numerous victims and serious economic retrogression as a result of large-scale destruction. And it would be unrealistic to suppose that the U.S. would allow other Cubas to develop in Latin America without interfering in any way. And even if a revolution in Colombia or anywhere else were to be successful in that the country were able to rid itself of its present rulers, economic progress would come to a standstill, because the U.S. would economically isolate the country, as it is at present doing to Cuba.

ALTERNATIVES TO VIOLENCE

Are there any alternatives? We must admit that far reaching structural changes have taken place in the 20th century. Many countries of the Third World have undergone a political revolution, or in any case a sudden political change, in the past decades. We must also admit that in most countries of the world there is a desire for renewal or for further, and in many cases fundamental changes in a large number of structures. Many of these countries are convinced, moreover, of man's ability to change many of these structures himself. This conviction is based partially on a knowledge of the results of science and technology.

We have seen that there are many characteristics as a result of which revolutionary situations may be engendered in accordance with the pattern of thought concerning revolution which has developed since 1789. The extraordinary thing is that patterns of thought are frequently extremely inflexible and change only with difficulty. This is also apparent from the analysis we have made of the phenomenon of revolution. The French Revolution has always served as a model for theories on revolution—this is borne out by 19th-century revolution, and in particular the Russian Revolution. The Chinese Revolution has added another important aspect, namely the militarized mass insurrection, a properly guided and well-planned revolution in which improvisation, a characteristic of the old-type revolution, played a much less significant part. Revolutionary theories and revolutionary behavior is continuing along these lines in Latin America.

The burning question is on what basis Christian churches should adopt these patterns of thought. Is it feasible to draw a parallel with the age-old influence of Greek philosophy on Christian and, to some extent, Islamic dogmatism? What scientific basis is there for the correctness and truth of these patterns of thought—using the word truth in the Hebrew sense of "reliability"?

We have seen that liberation and liberty are not necessarily concomitant states. Up to now they have never gone together in history where there was question of a social revolution. The question as to alternative possibilities is an urgent one, and its answer extremely difficult. It is not a scientific analysis of the phenomenon of revolution but a great deal of critical thought that is required here. This critical thinking could focus on the following possible alternatives of the historically developed pattern of revolution.

1. Technical improvements. These are accepted even by countries with a political structure which is unacceptable for most. If Marx is right—and he did discover an important truth here—this will change numerous other structures, such as instruction to produce technically skilled people, and, partly through this, the mentality and standard of living. As a result new organizational forms will come about, especially in the "economic sphere." These processes are slow, especially where governments are corrupt and do not fully cooperate. But if slowness in the historical process is inevitable, the transfer of technical accomplishments in a world in which international communication is daily increasing is certainly not small.

2. A change of the society implies a change in mentality and in patterns of thought. The existing revolutionary pattern involves indoctrination or—to use a less loaded term—education of the masses. Is not another kind of education than that which prepares for revolution possible? What are the possibilities of propaganda via the educational system and the press, and in so-called "closed" countries, via the radio?

3. What possibilities are offered by passive resistance? For many nonviolence has been buried with Martin Luther King. Is this a consequence of a revolutionary pattern of thought or are possibilities of passive resistance nonexistent? What possibilities does a general strike offer? The recent general strike in France almost resulted in political revolution. As it is, this strike is certain to bring about structural changes, notwithstanding its failure in other respects.

4. What are the possibilities of influencing members of the army and the police force in Latin America? This question again inquires into the possibilities of propaganda.

CONCLUSION

This report may have succeeded in substantiating our introductory proposition, namely that revolution is a burning problem and that whoever concerns himself with it is apt to burn his fingers. Scientific investigation of the problem has scarcely begun. Scientists are unable to say much at all on the subject. But it has become clear that the existing pattern of thought concerning revolution is extremely inflexible. Apparently changes in structures of thinking do not come about easily. Furthermore, this pattern has become very widespread, although this is no reflection on the degree of truth it contains. This could be a reason for the World Council of Churches breaking with the popular pattern of thought concerning the phenomenon of revolution. Perhaps it should do likewise with respect to the powers in control which are preventing structural changes.

This pattern of thought concerning the phenomenon of revolution does not take sufficiently into account the fact that there is polarity of tensions in every society, as a result of which the historical process can develop in many different directions. During the culminating point of the *Aufklärung,* Rousseau wrote about sentiments. During the Revolution there were both unlimited sentiments of "pitié pour le peuple malheureux" and tidal waves of aggression. At the same time the designers of the constitution, and later of the Code Civil, were convinced of the unrestricted value and applicability of this law as it was founded on human reason. Later, when romanticism, which based its philosophy on the organic processes of growth in history, occupied the minds and hearts of people, Guizot, wrote "A people straining to change its condition" is capable of doing so. This development is within the power of man (F. Guizot, *Histoire de la Civilisation en Europe,* 1838, first lecture). Reason and sentiment, manipulability and organic growth, *Aufklärung* and Romanticism, atheism and faith in God, are but a few examples of polarity. But when a spark jumps from one pole to another it is sometimes like a stroke of lightning: one pole is brightly illuminated while the other is unseen; at any rate later historians are easily misled. Their pattern of thought about history can even be determined by this.

We recommend, for the following reasons, use of the term "revolutionary transformation of the society." By using the term "transformation" one does not commit oneself to the customary pattern of thought on revolution, and keep a critical distance. But transformation does imply an overall change. The theme that God makes all things new can be expressed by it.

The addition "revolutionary" is necessary to indicate that the transformation and renewal are drastic. If rapid social change and a major break with antiquated institutions are wanted this word must be added. The word transformation alone will not attack sufficient credibility to the issue. Even De Gaulle speaks of "une grande imitation." Without the addition of this word many will not sufficiently trust that the churches are really prepared to line themselves up in the advance guard of those committed to the renewal of society.

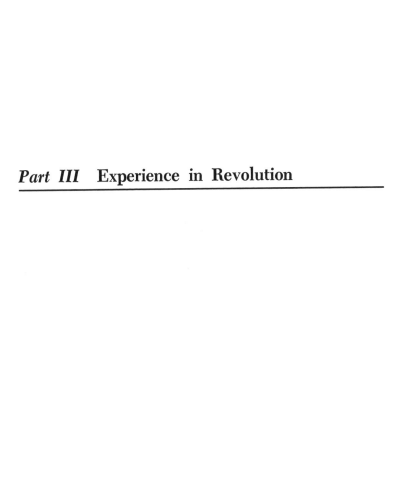

Part III Experience in Revolution

Chapter Eight The Stages of the Revolution in the Third World

Albert Paul Lentin

We have to look back somewhat in history if we want to understand the situation in which Western Europe finds itself vis-à-vis the Third World. If, rather arbitrarily, we take the Middle Ages as our starting point, we shall see that at that time there were many, variously distributed human societies that nevertheless had attained more or less equivalent cultural and economic levels. Great empires, like those of India, China and Mongolia, like the Arab empire of the Caliphs, or like the African empires of Mali and Ghana, were to all intents and purposes breeding grounds of civilizations that were just as brilliant, and perhaps better, than those of the societies of Western Europe of the same epoch. But at that time there began a movement of such extraordinary magnitude that even Marx, conditioned by a vision of his times that was not yet global, could only partly understand it. The spring was the inequality of economic development, key to all the problems of history, including contemporary history.

THE INEQUALITY OF ECONOMIC DEVELOPMENT

A "decalage" in the truest sense of the word began at that time, because the feudal system survived for many a long century within some societies, while in others it had already been abolished for some time. Without wanting to enter into the discussion about "Asian production methods," I would nevertheless like to recall that in Asia, for example, China remained in the throes of a particular kind of feudalism, while the concentration of power around the throne of the Mikado in Japan had the effect of breaking up the forces that opposed themselves to the arising of productive forces rather sooner than elsewhere. In the Arab world, the political and religious divisions regarding the interpretation of Islamic orthodoxy crystallized a series of late feudalisms, generators of decadence after the apogee of Arab greatness. In Western Europe, on the other hand, the centralized monarchies of Spain, England, France and Austria broke up the feudal structures more easily, thereby permitting the growth of the market economy and giving this region of the world the extraordinary fortune that it still enjoys today.

Mention must be made of a fact of the utmost importance, i.e., that the inequality of economic development, right from the very beginning, led to the exploitation of the less developed part of the world by the more developed one. While the ruling classes of monarchical, commercial and manufacturing Europe effected the first accumulation of capital through the intensive exploitation of a miserable peasantry, they loot America as soon as it is discovered (this is the rush for gold and spice by the conquistadores, the perpetrators of the Indian massacres) and quickly introduce Africa into the circuit of their exploitation. The Negro slave trade, for example, becomes part of the famous commercial triangle: bought in Africa in exchange for shoddy goods, the Negro slaves are sold to the plantation owners in America and the enormous profit of the operation returns to European parts, where ship owners and traders flourish. Thus, while some countries make their "mercantile revolution," others are paralyzed by the brake of feudalism.

The drama lies in the fact that every economic development brings others in its wake, while an initial underdevelopment only tends to become aggravated. The industrial revolution of the 19th century, the revolution of iron and steel, could come into being by starting from the accumulated capital and the technical know-how built up during the previous period; in the same way, the technological and scientific revolution of the second half of the 20th century, the revolution of the atom and of electronics, is only the daughter of the industrial revolution. An implacable logic ensures that the people who have lost the first opportunity will also lose the second and the third.

From the 15th century onwards the world has never ceased to live under an ever more brutal dichotomy, and the world seems increasingly like a pair of compasses whose two arms, development and underdevelopment, are continually coming to be wider apart. The law of the inequality of development, by virtue of which the societies that had the first impulse have enriched themselves at the expense of those that were behind or backward, has never ceased to impose itself from the 15th century onwards, thus accentuating the division between the two parts of the universe. Just as the explosion of the "mercantile revolution" is organically linked to the "triangular commerce" at the expense of the populations of Africa and South America and represents the first historical form of the "loot of the Third World," so the explosion of capitalism born from the "industrial revolution" is organically linked to colonial expansion, i.e., to the military conquest, to the political and cultural domination aimed at the permanent economic exploitation of the principal territories of Africa, Asia and South America by the "advanced" capitalist countries of Europe. Exploitation on the economic plane has taken place, and continues to take place, in accordance with the scheme of the "colonial pact" so perfectly described by Lenin: the "advanced" capitalist countries import the products and raw materials they need at low prices from the "backward" colonial countries and export to them their manufactured goods, which therefore find an easy and advantageous market in these countries.

Exceptional historical conditions during the 19th century began to turn the United States into the super power of the capitalist world; for example, there is the influx in a relatively short time of some 40 million emigrants in possession of European knowledge and techniques into a new territory extraordinarily rich in raw materials of every kind. The Spanish colonies in South America have no sooner freed themselves from the political tutelage of the mother country (the phenomenon of the

131

first decolonization) than they fall under the economic tutelage of the United States in full accordance with the characteristic mechanisms of the colonial pact, which function equally well in the political conditions of colonialism and in those of neocolonialism; they now suffer a continuation of the old dominations in a state of independence that is more theoretical than real.

THE SOCIALIST BREACH

In 1917 the October Revolution shakes the world; the capitalist system, which was becoming universal and seemed to extend its dominion over the entire globe, is peremptorily contested and is practically put into crisis over a goodly part of the world. A Socialist universe has come into being and for the last fifty years it has not ceased to develop. Its progress on the geographical level is marked by a number of milestones:

In 1945 there is a process of transformation that turns the semi-feudal countries of Eastern Europe into "popular democracies" after the war against Hitler; even an oppressive political system, the Stalinism copied from the Soviet model, does not prevent the impetuous economic development of these countries, at least during the early stages.

In 1949 there is the triumph of the Chinese Revolution. The example and the psychological influence of this revolution causes an upheaval of all political values in Asia, while the new Chinese strength consolidates that of two other anti-capitalist countries in Asia: North Korea and North Vietnam. In 1959 it is the turn of the Cuban Revolution to gain the upper hand.

However impressive this advance in a relatively short period of time may be, it must not make us forget that Socialism for the moment has done nothing more than open a breach in a worldwide universe that still remains essentially capitalist. The figures published by the United Nations are very revealing in this respect: 60% of world production comes from capitalist countries, but only 30% from Socialist countries (including China); only 10% comes from those areas that are now conventionally described as "countries of the Third World," a convenient but rather arbitrary terminology, because in practice the "Third World" is nothing other than the most exploited area of the capitalist world. The United Nations statistics also show that at least three quarters of world trade takes place between capitalist countries.

The weakness of Socialism vis-à-vis capitalism has for a certain period of time been hidden from the eyes of world opinion by the fact that the Soviet Union, at the price of a gigantic effort, has succeeded in catching and in certain cases overtaking the United States in some industrial "key sectors"; this made it possible for the Soviet Union to reach military parity with the United States from 1953 on (H-bomb, mass extermination weapons, intercontinental missiles) and to impose the "balance of terror"; but strategic and military equality does not yet mean economic equality.

Russia, which was initially very underdeveloped in spite of the fantastic progress she has since made (and this would seem to suggest that Socialism is the best way of overcoming underdevelopment), is still rather backward with respect to the United States in everything that concerns economic strength. Contrary to what some people try to maintain, the present world is not "bi-polar." Its principal pole is effectively to be found in the United States, because it is invariably the expansion of American imperialism that sets the most serious problems for humanity.

DECOLONIZATION AND "THIRD WORLDISM"

I have spoken of decolonization in connection with Latin America. What has been called "decolonization" was the radical and then victorious contestation by the colonial countries of the direct sovereignty of the colonizing countries; deep down in this phenomenon, at the level of the masses, there was a mute contestation of the foreign socio-cultural values imposed by the conqueror to further his political domination. The phenomenon, which developed in an impetuous manner after the end of the Second World War, first in Asia and then in Africa, came to an end about 1960. Classical colonialism, in fact, survives in some small sectors, such as the French "overseas departments," the "lust of the Caribbean," the "confetti of the Empire," or even the

Portuguese colonies in Africa, and this obliges the autochthonous population to struggle by means of guerrilla warfare against an archaic form of government.

A number of states were thus seen to emerge onto the scene of history between 1950 and 1960 that had not up to then had a true existence in the legal sense and have since chosen their own government, their diplomacy, an army, a flag of their own, a national anthem and their visiting card as members of the United Nations. Although independence in every case was granted rather than obtained by means of a national struggle, although this independence was (and, with a few exceptions, still is) more fictitious than real, the simultaneous appearance of these states has caused nearly everywhere, and even in the Western countries, a kind of "Afro-Asian" romanticism.

The very expression "Third World," perhaps primarily due to Professors Sauvy and Balandier who launched it in France at the time, expresses the concepts and the illusions of an epoch in which one tends to overvalue the specific weight of Asia, Africa and Latin America, not in a long-term vision (because this weight could one day become enormous), but rather in a vision of the more immediate destiny of humanity. The Bandung Conference in April 1955, with Pandit Nehru as its most famous and ardent propagandist, was wholly immersed in a "Third World" ideology. And yet this ideology is based on misunderstandings. In the spirit of some of its promoters the men of the three under-developed continents, these hungry, these backward, these "damned of the earth" represented a Third World comparable to the Third Estate created in France in 1789 against the nobility and the clergy who were swimming in abundance. The analogy, in truth, is rather superficial, because there are privileged people in the Third World, just as there are the miserable in "poor America" and in "poor Europe." According to other commentators the Third World represents a sector distinct from the other two, i.e., the Socialist world and the capitalist world.

For my part, I do not accept this classification; I think that the Third World does not exist as an economic or political reality. It exists only as a geographic entity, an easy phrase to designate the three continents of Asia, Africa and Latin America as one unit. On the political and economic level, what we call the Third World is nothing other than the part of the universe that is most exploited by the capitalist industrial world. This is so much true, for example, that when the Asian, African and Latin American member countries of the United Nations meet together within the ambit of the "group of the 71" in order to elaborate their common claims (Algiers conference, New Delhi conference), they can do nothing other than contest rather platonically a certain number of the fundamental laws of the operation of the capitalist system. Today we are rather a long way from the generous but confused doctrines of "Third Worldism" in 1955 and from this conception of the Third World as a third force on a world scale.

What, in fact, is the reality of these countries? It is principally characterized by a population increase that has become "accelerated," particularly as a result of the sanitary progress made in the 20th century with the liquidation of the great epidemics, vaccinations, preventive medicine, etc., and is at present reaching a 2% or 3% rate of growth per annum. The rate of economic growth certainly does not reach this figure in quite a number of countries of the Third World, and these would therefore have to be described as "nondeveloping countries." In other cases the economic explosion greatly exceeds the demographic explosion, at least according to statistics; but, in view of the fact that the unequal distribution of incomes ensures that this economic explosion should only go to the benefit of a minority of privileged people, the general evolution is characterized once again by diminishing living standards for the great majority of the population.

The number of countries in Asia, Africa and Latin America that can authentically be said to be "developing" can be counted on the fingers of one hand. All these countries are "underdeveloping" because they belong to the capitalist universe. The only two exceptions are China and Cuba, which have carried out a large-scale collectivization of the means of production and exchange and are also the only countries that can be described as socialist in the technical sense of the word. These two are also the only ones who have "taken off," if I may use a term dear to economists; the others remain more or less underdeveloped, and the most fitting term for describing them would surely be "over-exploited countries."

SOCIALISM AND UNDERDEVELOPMENT

The observations I have just made induce me to give some rapid consideration to the problem of socialism and underdevelopment before I return to give further consideration to the situation of the Third World within the capitalist universe.

Although the "Socialist" label is rather fashionable in the Third World (there is talk of African Socialism, Islamic Socialism, etc.), we can hardly content ourselves with these words or consider as "socialist" certain experiences that are called such merely because they appeal to certain policy recipes, but in actual practice adapt themselves to the fundamental realities of neo-capitalism. Rather must we carefully follow the cases, few as they are, of some countries in Africa and Asia, the so-called "revolutionary countries" (Syria, U.A.R., Algeria, Guinea, Mali, Brazzaville Congo, Tanzania), who try to approach socialism in successive stages, choosing the "noncapitalist road to development" at home and, at the external level, trying to break the neo-colonialist circuits on which they still depend by progressively diversifying their trade and seeking greater links with the socialist industrial countries.

Here, once again, we must remain lucid and not lose sight of the fact that the socialist world cannot do a great deal for these pioneer countries of the Third World. As already mentioned, the fundamental reason for this impotence is the weakness of the socialist world in the industrial field in its economic competition with the capitalist world. Undoubtedly, the assistance that the socialist countries can give to the countries of the Third World is really more valid than the pseudo-help of the capitalist countries, which basically reduces itself to the export of capital. The socialist countries offer long-term financial credits at limited rates of interest and, above all, they expect to be repaid

136

in goods produced thanks to their technical assistance; in this way they promote the industrialization of the underveloped countries, whereas the capitalist countries practically put a brake on this process. All the same, because their means are limited, their efforts can only be made in specific cases and cannot be very far-reaching, even though there are some very remarkable examples. I am thinking, for example, of the links that have been created between the U.S.S.R. and Cuba, links that make it possible for the Cubans to sell their sugar in a stable market and at an advantageous price.

There is another phenomenon that limits the effects of possible interventions by the socialist industrial countries in the Third World: the socialist countries have for the greater part passed directly from feudalism to socialism without having gone through the long intermediate stages of bourgeois democracy and expanding capitalism, particularly colonial capitalism, and they do not consequently have sufficient personnel with long-standing and direct experience of Asia and Africa such as the Western European countries have. Their "technical assistants" and their diplomats must therefore go through an apprenticeship in the countries of the Third World, and this makes them liable to fall into psychological errors due to their limited knowledge of local conditions.

Furthermore, within the socialist countries themselves, the problems of the Third World are only of partial interest to public opinion, which is almost entirely taken up by their own more or less resolved problems: the modernization of the economy, the introduction of new management methods, liberty of expression and the other individual liberties.

Lastly, the principal merit of the socialist countries (and particularly the U.S.S.R.) in the eyes of the dynamic forces of Asia, Africa and Latin America is the fact that they exist, and their limited economic possibilities are always interesting, above all their military strength. The armed force of the Soviet Union to a large extent stops and contains the aggressiveness of American imperialism, and it is only within the security provided by this military defence that revolutions can develop, as has already been done to some extent by certain revolutions (the Cuban Revolution, for example) that would have been suffocated without the defence of Soviet arms.

Without calling this fact into doubt, certain revolutionaries in the Third World, particularly in Latin America, complain that the solidarity shown for them by the U.S.S.R. and the European socialist countries is limited by the problem of "peaceful co-existence" between East and West. The peaceful co-existence generated by the "balance of terror," and which is primarily a nuclear co-existence, is in itself an expression of the precarious equilibrium between socialism and capitalism. The principal communist parties in the world, who voted a joint resolution at the end of their meeting at Moscow in November 1960, as well as the representatives of the U.S.S.R., China and the Asian, African and Latin American revolutionary movements assembled on the occasion of the Conference of the Three Continents in January 1966, have stressed that this "peaceful co-existence" will not be in a position to put the brake on either the class struggle in the capitalist countries or the struggles for liberation in the countries of the Third World. In fact, the entire debate turns on the interpretation of this principle: the Soviets tend to limit every commitment that might bring them into a direct confrontation with the Americans and a thermonuclear apocalypse; but many revolutionaries of the Third World reproach them for not taking sufficient "calculated risks" to help the anti-imperialist struggle, and the guerrilla struggles in particular.

THE CONTRADICTIONS OF THE GREAT BLOCS

Let us now examine the problems of capitalism and the Third World. In general it may be said that the era we have now entered is an era of neo-colonialism. We are living in an epoch in which American and European capitalism accepts the sovereignty of independent but often rather small states almost throughout the Third World, because Africa has been "Balkanized" just as Latin America was during an earlier stage. But they maintain the old system of the "colonial pact" with slight adaptations; the industrial countries continue to sell their manufactured goods at ever increasing prices and to buy the "basic products" of the countries of the Third World for less and less, this being particularly true in the case of raw materials such as copper from Zambia and Chile, tin from Bolivia, oil from Venezuela, bananas from Honduras, iron from Liberia, bauxite from Guinea, cacao from Ghana, ground nuts from Senegal, etc. The economic domination, and to a large extent also the cultural domination of the capitalist countries is thus strongly maintained in the three underdeveloped continents. Only the political domination has been transformed; it now passes through the mediation of the autochthonous feudal or bourgeois classes.

I have already mentioned the serious and continually increasing disparity between the development of the industrial countries and the nonindustrial ones; the proportion was six to one in 1952, but in 1967 the per capita national product of the European countries was nine times greater than that of the underdeveloped countries. In this connection I have also suggested the image of a large compass whose arms are continually moving apart. One might add that inside the large compass, on the side of the underdevelopment arm, there is a secondary compass behaving in the same manner: because the privileged regularly increase their profits, while in the greater part of the cases the mass of the population sees its living standards diminish just as regularly.

Refusing to admit that underdevelopment is only the other face of an over-exploitation for the benefit of the Western world (U.S.A. and Europe), some theoreticians maintain that the fundamental antagonism in the contemporary universe ought to be found in the opposition between the developed countries, irrespective of their regime, and the underdeveloped countries (again irrespective of their political or economic orientation). According to these people the principal contradiction is no longer to be found in the contradiction between East and West, but rather between North and South; in other words, the contradiction between the Northern hemisphere, where the greater part

139

of the industrial countries are concentrated, and the Southern hemisphere which contains the majority of the nonindustrial countries.

I think that an interpretation of this kind does not give an exact picture of reality or, at the very best, only gives a very partial one. It is quite true that the industrial countries have many points in common, even though their economies are different. It is also true that the differences of economic and social level in China and the Soviet Union have led to the conflicts between these two great socialist countries in spite of their common ideology. Although this contradiction must not be underestimated, it seems to me to be quite secondary when compared to the principal contradiction, which always remains that between capitalism and socialism; today, just as yesterday, capitalism is the decisive and permanent factor in the exploitation that generates underdevelopment.

Outside Europe we find that the Chinese leaders are the ones to put greater emphasis on the priority that should be given to the opposition between rich countries and poor countries (including Russia), between the "proprietor nations" and the "proletarian nations," and this tendency has only increased with the passing of the years. At the Conference of the Three Continents in January 1966 the Chinese delegates, although somewhat reticently, were still prepared to find an agreement with the Soviets regarding a common concept of "peaceful co-existence." But they quickly went back on the compromise and today they assert that the revolutionary struggle is confined to the Chinese and their friends on one side, and the "modern revisionists of the U.S.S.R. allied with American imperialism" on the other. This thesis may possibly satisfy Peking's neo-nationalism and the ideological extremism of the "cultural revolution," but it finds little response in the Third World, particularly during the last two or three years. Although the countries of the Third World may be irritated by the Soviet concept of "peaceful co-existence," which is too restrictive and egoistical for their liking, almost all the revolutionaries of the Third World refuse to put the Soviet Union, a natural, if not always completely faithful ally for them, into the

140

same category as the United States; the latter remain the No. 1 enemy, the principal exploiter, corrupter and exterminator of the people of the Third World.

CAPITALIST FORMS OF GROWTH AND SOCIOECONOMIC EQUILIBRIUMS

How does the underdeveloped world come to be penetrated and dominated by American capitalism? The answer may vary slightly according to the different countries of the Third World in whom the United States is interested, but fundamentally the pattern always remains the same. The government of the U.S.A. maintains and imposes the political power of the local oligarchies, particularly in Latin America, quite irrespective of whether these be the old landed aristocracy or the new commercial and industrial bourgeoisie, which is in any case closely linked with the land owners. While the most archaic structures of society continue to exist, American private capital is invested where it can make the greatest and most readily repatriated profits; it has been calculated that one American dollar employed in Latin America produces a profit of three dollars within the space of two years.

The most profitable sectors for Yankee capitalist expansion are mining and oil extraction, at least from the structural point of view; in the geographical sense they are to be found in the areas closest to the coast and the great lines of communication, because this facilitates the rapid shipping of the "basic products." These regions are also the ones to which the Americans prefer to send their manufactured goods and where they try to stimulate the consumption needs of a part of the population in order to enlarge their export market; these areas thus become "growth poles," epicenters of undoubted development—development that is neither global nor harmonious, but rather artificial and harmful in the long run, because it accentuates the unbalance within the country itself.

French colonial capitalism once achieved fame by artificially developing the Algerian coastal regions at the expense of the "bled" in the interior, which was abandoned and sacrificed.

American capitalism is now repeating a similar process on a much vaster scale in Latin America, and is creating an ever-growing cleft, as for example in Peru, between the privileged coast and the interior mountains, refuge of the miserable Indians; or, as in Brazil, between the rich "industrial triangle" Rio de Janeiro-São Paolo-Belo Herizonte and the tragic northwest, the "polygon of drought," land of thirst and death.

This "unequal development" under the impulse of American capitalism has effects on the social plane that can be found also in other areas of the Third World (with few exceptions), and particularly throughout Latin America. This type of development has the effect of creating a whole category of privileged, a complete "commercial bourgeoisie," which prospers around the "development poles" and in the furrow of American expansion, but on account of its dependence is quite incapable of constituting itself as a "national bourgeoisie" and can only supply the Americans with the technical and political personnel needed for this "geared domination." This kind of development also slowly brings into being an ambiguous working class that has stable employment and a guaranteed income, and is therefore undoubtedly privileged when compared to the "damned of the land," the poor and permanently unemployed peasants of the shanty towns; but at the same time it is a pauperized working class, because the looting of the various countries by the American monopolies and the corresponding currency devaluations, ineluctably followed by price increases, work toward a general impoverishment of the population (including the working class) of which only the ruling oligarchy can steer clear. Moreover, the stability of employment for the workers is rather relative, because the industries created by the Americans provide little work, while the spectre of unemployment is always present and the existence of an enormous mass of unemployed permits the national or foreign employers to exercise a ready pressure on wage levels. In economic conditions of this kind the condition of the working class (in a country like Brazil, for example) recalls that of the European proletariat in the 19th century: inexorable exploitation, starvation wages, below-cost labor competition from women and children, etc.).

The unequal development that causes the profitable productive sectors to progress, but leaves an agriculture that is still closely controlled by the land owners and *latifondista* in a state of complete immobility, brings a catastrophic situation in the countryside. The landed proprietors leave much land uncultivated and the land they decide to exploit is badly cultivated; agricultural production therefore progresses very slowly. In these conditions the inexorable demographic growth adds hundreds of thousands to the number of agricultural workers that are treated like medieval serfs; but it also increases the number of landless peasants, often the sons of former small proprietors who have been expropriated by various means by the owners of the large estates. These peasants are not only the hungriest, but also the most "offended and humiliated." The unequal development produces a rural exodus without precedents, because the "hunger migration" each year pushes hundreds of thousands of the rural population, the future unemployed, towards the sordid peripheries of the towns, the "poverty belt" of the metropolitan cities that are the "growth poles." Shanty towns spring up like true tumors around each capital; if 51% of the Latin American population has now become urbanized, 14% of the citizens lives in shanty towns and in indescribable conditions. The most frightening shanty towns in Africa and Asia, those of Casablanca, Constantina and Dakar, are luxurious quarters when compared to the *favelas* of Rio or Recife, the *barriadas* of Lima or the *ranchites* of Caracas.

WHY REFORMISM IS IMPOSSIBLE

How can such a situation be overcome? The reformist road chosen by Chile and in a rather less clear manner also by Venezuela, Peru and Colombia, starts from the fundamental idea of integration. The reformists think that a relatively planned state, by means of a particular effort (priority capital investments in sectors that are not yet profitable, progressive changes in agrarian structures, etc.), can produce an appreciable development of the archaic, backward pre-capitalist and previously abandoned areas of a given country and thus "integrate" them progressively into the modern capitalist universe and "homogenize" the economy.

The American administration at the time of Kennedy took up this doctrine; it launched the great project of the Alliance for Progress and spent considerable sums to help some "democratic" Latin American governments in this endeavor. The new system, however, did not greatly modify the fundamental mechanisms of the looting of Latin America by the U.S.A.; but, inasmuch as it placed the accent on the need for public credits from Washington for the construction of roads, schools and hospitals in Latin America, it was rather more ductile and astute than the previous administrations. The undertaking was disappointing in practice. The greater part of the officials charged with putting Kennedy's plans into practice were tied up with the local oligarchies, and in too many cases their choice in the distribution of the manna was inspired by corruption rather than the public interest; millions of dollars were wasted. In the end the failure of the Alliance for Progress was admitted even in Washington; Congress has now returned to its old "McCarthyism" and at the summit conference of the Organization of American States in April 1967 Lyndon Johnson avoided any promise of help from the American Treasury to the various Latin American governments. In these conditions it is very difficult to see what means might enable the "reformist" leaders to maintain their promises to develop the backward sectors of the countries they govern.

In any case, these leaders are not even capable of making their own fundamental decisions. They can do nothing but negotiate with Washington from positions of weakness; and one cannot see how Washington might modify a policy of expansion and domination that corresponds to the inner logic of its capitalist system and leads to the distortion rather than the "integration" of the Latin American economies. This factual situation blocks any concrete possibilities of a reformism that may put forward interesting theories, but which in practice is condemned to impotence.

These contestations are based not only on theory, but also on the simple observation of reality. It is quite impossible to find a single example in either Asia, Africa or Latin America of a country that has achieved a harmonious development by following the free play of capitalism. The only case that might be open to discussion is that of the Ivory Coast, which undoubtedly has seen a spectacular rise; but when we examine the phenomenon more closely, and we can do this, for example, by reading the recent and well-documented book *Le Miracle Ivoirien* by the economist Samir Amin, we shall see that this development is principally the result of the rational and intensive exploitation of agricultural crops in great demand on the world market and therefore capable of bringing a lot of money into the country's coffers; but this has not prevented the aggravation of the unbalance among the various economic sectors, nor the accentuation of the diversification and the antagonism of the social classes within the country.

THE SOVIET LINE AND THE CUBAN LINE

The heaviest capitalist domination is perhaps that of the United States. Although the U.S.A. population does not represent more than 6% of the world population, the United States is responsible for 33% of the total industrial production and controls from 60 to 80% of such key sectors as electronics, the chemical industry, the oil industry, machine tools and motor cars. For the whole world, but particularly for the Third World, the "American Challenge" brings to the foreground the problems of the struggle against the hegemony of the U.S.A.

American capitalism is bent on a permanent expansion in all directions, because it is more concentrated, more militarized and better armed on the technical plane than any other capitalism. It stimulates the consumption needs of its own population in order to create new outlets on the internal market. As regards the less evolved capitalist countries, the United States, thanks to

145

their better technological condition and the "brain drain" (a loot of foreign brains in order to be able to utilize the discoveries of the scientists and specialists attracted to the United States), can put the economies of their allied countries into a state of vassalage by obtaining control of their key sectors. As we have already indicated, the looting of the Third World by the United States is taking place in accordance with the mechanism of the "colonial pact." The socialist and anti-imperialist governments of the entire world are agreed in giving absolute priority to the struggle against such an attempt at global domination, but we must not lose sight of the fact that there are divergencies among them as regards the roads and methods to follow in this struggle.

The U.S.S.R. and its European allies are in favor of a global strategy and take account of the fact that the underdeveloped countries as yet play a secondary part in the destiny of the world. Although they represent 52% of the world's surface and 42% of its population, they only produce 11.5% of the total product and this is less than half of the U.S.A. production. According to the Soviets, the fundamental objective that must never be lost from sight in these conditions is the progressive transformation of the general relationship of forces in the universe, until such time as the socialist world becomes stronger than the capitalist world, thereby accentuating the internal contradictions and crises of the latter. In this general framework, therefore, the strengthening of the "socialist camp" is more decisive than the development of this or that revolutionary struggle in the various parts of the Third World.

When seen in this light there must be a resolute defence of the "peaceful co-existence" that manifests itself today, and this not only because it safeguards the world against the danger of a nuclear apocalypse, but also because it is useful for the socialist countries; on the economic and technical level they are still inferior to the more developed capitalist countries and they therefore have every interest in increasing the exchanges of every kind with these countries as this will enable them to accelerate some intermediate development stages, make up the lag and reduce the distance that separates them from the capitalist world.

146

According to the Soviet leaders and their allies in Eastern Europe, the progressive movements in the Third World ought to understand that there is nothing more important (even for themselves) than the strengthening of the potential of the "socialist camp," because the attainment of a stronger position will enable it to shake the tutelage of American capitalism in other parts of the world, to change the old-establishment economic circuits and to subtract countries from the influence of the United States; this has already happened in Cuba, and to some extent also in Syria and the U.A.R.

This *Weltanschauung* also requires the revolutionaries of the Third World to understand that if the "national bourgeoisie" in certain Latin American countries, for example, shows ambitions of independence, then the U.S.S.R. must help them within the limits of its means, show them that they are not left completely alone to face the United States and demonstrate by means of a visible presence (financial and technical assistance) that certain alternatives are possible, even though these governments may be fighting against guerrilla movements, as is the case in Venezuela or Colombia. In the socialist world this policy is opposed not only by the particular concepts of the Chinese, but also by those of North Vietnam, North Korea and Cuba. I do not think that one can here speak of a "third road to communism," because the North Vietnamese in particular assert that their long-term objective is that of uniting the U.S.S.R. and China in the struggle against the U.S.A. and a special ideology would only complicate this future reconciliation. I incline to think that it would be more proper to speak of a political and psychological "third tendency," that of three small countries that have been sensitized by the manifestations of the "great power chauvinism" and by all the attempts at "satellitization."

On the other hand, these three small countries are in the forefront of the anti-imperialist struggle, and they are therefore quite naturally among those who more readily incline towards that revolutionary radicalism so clamorously expressed by "Che" Guevara; a radicalism that is based on the refusal of every opportunist "accommodation" with bourgeois governments, even in the name of "superior imperatives" of global strategy, on a deliberate voluntary dedication, a moral and political search for the "new man," a refusal of "material stimulants" and an appeal to the "ideological stimulants" for the construction of socialism. The theoreticians of the "third tendency" maintain that if the miserables of the Third World are to be freed from their exploited and oppressed condition and from their backwardness so as to ensure the development of their social, political and cultural personality, and also from their religious backwardness (as say those who are believers), one has to conduct an implacable struggle without any tactical compromises against the very structures that suffocate them: the capitalist neo-colonial structures superimposed on the old pre-capitalist structures represented by feudalism and tribalism.

A Necessary Awakening

This broadly drawn picture of the past and the present permits me to suggest a reply to the question that has been implicit in the whole of my exposition: Are there any objective revolutionary conditions in the Third World? I reply "yes" without any hesitation, because the present conditions of the Third World are such that only the road of the most radical contestation, including armed contestation in certain cases, can make it come out of the state of underdevelopment. The real emancipation of the underdeveloped countries passes through the elimination of the imperial and neo-colonial mortgage, through the fundamental transformation of the social and economic structures, the agrarian revolution (and not a circumstantial and limited agrarian reform), through the destruction of the big estates, the liberation of the productive forces of the countryside, the introduction of millions of landless peasants into creative circuits, the utilization of the "primitive accumulation of capital" created in this way by the modernization of agriculture for the purpose of winning the battle for an autonomous industrialization and, lastly (for all these formidable tasks), the "human investment," the political, psychological, moral and spiritual mobilization of the population that will have to be put to work for the success of these great changes. One will have to admit that a historical revolution of this kind, which I consider to be ineluctable, will not be made without a great deal of "blood, sweat and tears" and that it will be very slow at the start, even if it will accelerate later.

Is it possible in the immediate future to foresee revolutionary explosions of great import or particularly efficient revolutionary actions in the Third World? I don't think so, but I believe that in the course of the next ten or fifteen years these explosions and these actions will continually grow in size, until they become sufficiently massive to affect the destiny of mankind in a decisive rather than a marginal manner. The revolutionaries who (as Engels says) "would like to turn their impatience into theory" will be irritated by hearing me predict the relative slowness of a process that they would like to see very rapid and which they announce as being almost immediate; at the same time, the pharisees and the righteous among the privileged of the industrial world will cover their faces before the prospect of these assaults and these upheavals that are undoubtedly rather drastic, but historically necessary and morally desirable, but which they prefer to ignore, call into doubt or deny. For my own part, I feel I must agree with the forecast of an inevitable and long "escalation of violence" whose first steps are only now being taken. I believe that I can base this forecast on the analysis of a phenomenon that seems to be of crucial importance in connection with the Third World: the phenomenon of the awakening.

After having forgotten the frightening realities of the Third World with supreme indifference for many decades, European and North American public opinion is now discovering them almost on the spur of the moment and with great surprise. But "hunger in the world," even though it may now be considerably aggravated by an unprecedented demographic growth, is not a new problem. The 19th century stood under the sign of the great famines in Asia, particularly in India and China, in Latin America, in Africa and right up to the doorsteps of Europe. These catastrophes did not then arouse anything other in Europe or the

United States than the testimonies of a few missionaries, and the press of Paris, London and New York dealt with them in just a few lines. The drama of famine, undernourishment, underemployment, illiteracy, primitive housing conditions and, more generally, the atrocious poverty of the populations of the Third World, all these are now very widely known. The growing awareness of this drama among an ever increasing number of Americans and Europeans, in spite of their natural egotism, causes the privileged to have an undoubted guilty conscience, although this guilty conscience tends to express itself through the reflexes of a paternal or fraternal charity, rather than through a search for justice. Those who do seek justice and who have a generous soul often commit a particular error. The American, and even more so the European, who brutally discovers how many of his kind in Africa, Asia, and Latin America are living in subhuman conditions is led to think that these "damned of the earth" will rebel very soon, because he imagines that in this same situation he would rebel immediately. But such a vision, for lack of first-hand knowledge of the concrete realities of the Third World, does not take account of the incredible burden of resignation and fatalism that weighs upon the most miserable societies by virtue of illiteracy, cultural backwardness and obscurantism. This fantastic force of inertia has not even been taken into account by otherwise valid theoreticians of the emancipation of the Third World who believed themselves able to assert that the poor peasant classes in Asia, Africa and Latin America were already revolutionary, although in actual fact they are only potentially and virtually revolutionary.

There is, however, a new fact: for some years past an as yet slow but growing awakening has begun to shake the passivity of the masses of the Third World. The face of the Third World is now rapidly changing. The development of the means of transport seems to shorten distances and shrink the world; the education, or at least the primary education, that in spite of everything is now being given to a growing number of youngsters, as well as the more rapid and better diffusion of news and information, is now awakening the spirits. The peasants who can listen to transistor sets even in the most out-of-the-way countryside are slowly becoming politically conscious. The rural exodus that drives millions of uprooted peasants into the towns also permits these pariahs to measure the distance between their miserable fate and the provocative opulence of the privileged, a distance they had not hitherto been able to imagine. All these phenomena provoke changes in depth and although it is not yet possible to say when these will arrive at complete maturation, we can nevertheless be sure that they will end up by provoking irresistible and irreversible upheavals.

In my opinion, we have to consider the popular wars of liberation that are now taking place in Vietnam, in Laos, and to a lesser extent in Portuguese Guinea, in this perspective; but it also seems to me that we must consider the more modest guerrilla activities in some countries such as Thailand, Palestine, Angola, Mozambique, Guatemala, Venezuela and Colombia in the same perspective. The total number of active guerrilla fighters does not at present exceed a few thousand, and these rebels do not for the present seriously menace the repressive military and police apparatus of states in fief to imperialism. Nevertheless, if guerrilla warfare constitutes only a marginal phenomenon on the strategic plane, it can be considered as a more substantial phenomenon on the political level. In fact, it has some spectacular and often romantic aspects and tends to crystallize sentiments among the masses that were previously latent and confused; perhaps this crystallization is primarily sentimental, but it is intense. At the popular level it also brings into being the poem, the legend (for example the legend of Che Guevara or Camilo Torres), the *chanson de geste* and all this represents the first step toward political consciousness. It is anti-imperialist and anti-capitalist and therefore makes it known in the country where it takes place that colonialism has become neo-colonialism, and that the enemy of the oppressed is not only the foreigner who more or less controls the economy of the country, but also the privileged "national" who helps the oppressor's domination to take root.

Among all the poor (and those who feel solidarity with them) who are affected by guerrilla warfare there is only a small minority who decide to join the guerrillas and, undoubtedly, to die with arms in their hands, rather than to die of hunger and poverty; but, true as this may be, the others radicalize their struggle in politics, in the trade unions and the universities.

The awakening that is now taking place is not a substitute for systematic and minute political work at the base, but it prepares and facilitates this work. The losses in the ranks of the guerrilla fighters are very heavy, and the underground at the moment (to use an expression that may be cruel but exact) is only a "missionary underground" and few of its members will survive; but for this very reason the "mission" will have an intense force of irradiation within a few years. The message will continue to be transmitted and will grow in effectiveness, because "those who fall" will be replaced by a sufficient number of those who "come out of the shade," and these will be sufficiently numerous not only to replace the first volunteers killed with arms in their hands, but also to ensure that the movements of armed insurrection will make slow, but nevertheless consistent progress.

Towards the Deadline of 1980

Asia, the poorest and also the most restless of the underdeveloped continents where China's giant shadow is making itself felt, and Latin America, where hate of the "gringo" has become a natural and spontaneous sentiment of the masses everywhere, will be in the forefront of the "long march" towards total and radical contestation of the general capitalist system directed by the United States, even though this march will develop in different conditions on the various continents.

Che Guevara, in his message to OSPAAL of April 6, 1967, was able to say of Africa that for the moment it was "an almost virgin continent for the neo-colonial invasion," and Africa will certainly find itself outstripped by the position of Asia or Latin America. This continent, in fact, is underpopulated because for long centuries it was regularly cleaned out by the slave trade; today it only counts 330 million inhabitants, while there are 250 million inhabitants in Latin America in a territory of only half the size of Africa. But it is also only half as developed as Latin

America, having been particularly thoroughly looted by the mechanisms of the "deterioration in the terms of trade." This process gradually impoverishes the socially most disinherited categories, and particularly the peasant class which constitutes 87% of the continent's population; in a more or less distant future there will inevitably be increasingly serious conflicts that will oppose the masses to the bureaucratic middle classes that are now prospering around the administrative apparatuses of these small and artificial states of "Balkanized" Africa. The social classes in Africa are still only in an embryonic state and the class struggle will not therefore have the same sense and the same content that it has in Europe; but it is a sure part of the future.

At what moment willl the clash with the neo-capitalist system break out on a world scale subsequent to the general crisis of imperialism or at least its first manifestations? It seems to me that one might think in terms of the years between 1975 and 1980. Why this deadline? I am inclined to think that this approximate date will see the multiplication of the disorders provoked by hunger and the various phenomena that cause the deficiencies of the Third World will reach a maximum. This date will also presumably coincide with an extensive affirmation of the Latin American guerrilla wars; here we cannot by any means exclude the possibility of a Brazilian guerrilla war, a guerrilla war that will undoubtedly have a strong Christian characterization and which, if it breaks out and develops, will exercise an enormous influence; it will be taking place in an immense country with 85 million inhabitants, rich in natural resources and economic possibilities of every kind.

At the same time we must not forget that the U.S.S.R. will also have considerably strengthened its economic and military potential and will therefore be able to intervene more effectively in certain parts of the Third World, and particularly in the Middle East where the world imperialist system is presently reaping fabulous profits from the exploitation of oil. The Peking government, which will increasingly dominate the Asian scene, will have made alarming progress with its atomic and missile potential. The progress that China has made in this field in the space

153

of a few years is so astonishing as to make one reasonably think that, in spite of the "anti-missile missile" network that the U.S.A. has now begun to install on its territory, she will by then have intercontinental missiles with thermo-nuclear warheads capable of striking San Francisco and New York. The strategic superiority that presently permits the Americans to keep the Chinese at bay —for fear of nuclear destruction the Chinese are not making any move in spite of their verbal extremism—will by then have diminished to such an extent that the "deterrent" will no longer be in favor of the U.S.A.; in fact, the U.S.A. is far more vulnerable because the population is only a quarter that of China and the principal resources are concentrated in comparatively small spaces. This reversal of power relationships will permit a multiplication of revolutionary uprisings, this time directly supported by China, and will lead to the gradual liquidation of American influence in Asia, a breach having already been made by the defeat in Vietnam. Moreover, the American ruling classes will find themselves faced more dramatically than today by the two insoluble problems represented by the revolt of more than twenty million Negroes and by the confused but vehement contestation by the new generation and a large part of the intellectuals of the values of the economic society and the traditional ethics of a purely formal democracy.

The combined effect of these different but simultaneous phenomena, in my opinion, could be felt during the period 1975-1980 and thus reveal the first signs of the general crisis of a capitalism that has arrived at its "supreme stage," i.e. imperialism. This crisis, once begun, will last for several decades and will develop only slowly. The general revolution of the Third World is certainly not a fact of tomorrow, but at the end of this analysis I think that one can conclude that all the objective revolutionary conditions are already present and becoming more accentuated in the countries of the Third World and are preparing the irreversible upheavals of the future.

154

Chapter Nine Latin America—Land of Revolution

CHRISTIANS ARE COMPELLED TO CHOOSE

The conviction that Latin America must pass through a profound and rapid reform of its social, economic and political structures if it is to be capable of feeding, educating and employing its two hundred million inhabitants, which will be four hundred before the end of the century, is probably the only conviction unanimously held by all Latin Americans. This view is not only expressed by the left, which in any case is not in power anywhere in the continent if exception be made of Cuba; even the parties of the right use a revolutionary language; the Brazilian military government presents itself as revolutionary; Ongania in the Argentine declares that he is carrying through the necessary revolution; Barrientos in Bolivia likes to pass himself off as a revolutionary . . . and so on.

President Kennedy once declared that Latin America stood in need of a true revolution; such a statement coming from John Kennedy may have seemed quite a natural thing to many people in view of the open-mindedness and political sensitivity of the late President; but when Lyndon Johnson himself urges a revolution in the Latin American continent, then however surprising this may seem, we are really faced by unanimity.

The voice of the Church adds itself to the voice of the politicians. The Latin American hierarchy expressed itself in the same sense in the course of the meeting of its episcopal council (CELAM) held at Mar de la Plata two years ago. The position did not change recently at Meddlin. An ever growing number of bishops insists on the same individual diagnosis: fundamental reforms, urgent, rapid and far-reaching, are absolutely necessary to liberate the masses of the continent from misery, hunger and ignorance. Protestant ministers, either in groups or individually, express the same opinion. Fortunately, this unanimity does not deceive anybody. But the very success of the word revolution and the other terms and expressions that mean more or less the same thing does seem to indicate that the present situation in Latin America is so serious and so abnormal that there are very few people who dare to pronounce themselves clearly in favor of maintaining it.

The "revolution" of the powerful, the land owners and, more generally, of all those who benefit from the status quo is evidently nothing other than a project of superficial reforms designed for the precise purpose of drawing the teeth of those forces that would be capable of unleashing a true revolutionary or even reformist process. It is the revolution of those who are calculatedly sensitive to the warning of the encyclical *Populorum Progressio*, especially the passage in which the Pope reminds the rich of the risks they run by not granting the necessary reforms. Then there are those who sincerely call for true reforms, but without in any way implying a replacement of the existing structure; in these they see nothing other than abuses or operational defects, and they therefore consider a simple correction to be sufficient. There is another position that diagnoses the evils of Latin American society as structural evils that cannot be removed without a reform of the structures themselves. We may already say that this position is revolutionary for the very reason that it calls for the reform of the structures themselves and not only for reforms within the existing structures.

The element that permits us to make a significant distinction between the various revolutionary groups within the very wide definition that we have given to them consists of their respective choice of means. The orthodox Communist Parties in Latin America, all of which maintain their obedience to Moscow, increasingly give the impression of having chosen the "democratic and parliamentary road"; they are therefore pacifists and legalists, although they never fail to claim to be the vanguard of the revolutionary movement. Fidel Castro unceasingly denounces and condemns this position assumed by the various Latin American Communist Parties. But there are also those who have lost the illusion of being able to achieve profound reforms without power passing effectively to another class; certain that this passage of power will not be possible except through an organized struggle that the prompt reaction of the present holders of power will force to be a violent one, these groups have decided in favor of an immediate armed struggle, and particularly guerrilla warfare, as the only revolutionary road in Latin America. Fidel Castro, Che Guevara and Camilo Torres are the best-known representatives of this tendency.

The debate on violence is in the first place a debate on "Christianity and violence," and this means that it is primarily being carried on by Christian groups. There can be no doubt that this debate, apparently a theological one, is in practice based on ideology. There are therefore groups that declare themselves to be for the acceptance or the refusal of violence. Among those who define themselves as non violent there is Dom Helder Camara, who enjoys great influence over Latin American public opinion and today leads a movement that originally called itself "Pressao moral libertadora" and assumed the title of "Action for Justice and Peace" after the Bogota Congress. The nonviolence of Dom Helder seems to be instinctive and sentimental, but it is also based on considerations of a tactical order; on the one hand he justifies it with his own inability to kill, on the other he deduces it from an analysis of the particular situation of international politics. This means that Dom Helder will at least be able to admit guerrilla warfare as morally and historically justified if the circumstances change. The position of another group, which also has its representatives among the Latin American episcopate, is that of leaving the responsibility for judging the effectiveness at a given historical moment of an armed defence against an already existing "institutionalized violence" to individuals and political movements. The position of this group is characterized by the clarity with which they denounce this violence of the rich and at the same time justify the right of the poor to defend themselves against it, even though the only effective means to this end may be armed struggle. But there are also those who insist on saying that it is obvious that violence is anti-Christian, against the spirit of the Gospels, even when it is a case of reacting to institutionalized violence. They always base themselves on the encyclical *Populorum Progressio* and above all the recent speeches made by Paul VI, according to which institutionalized violence, i.e. the violence of the rich who instrumentalize the state, the law, the army and the police, is always a lesser evil than the violence of the revolutionary movement, in other words the violence of the poor who are completely deprived of any other effective means of defence.

The positions we have mentioned above are representative of more or less large sections of Latin Americans, but they are usually expressed by some significant representatives, irrespective of whether these be individually engaged men or groups; it is therefore interesting to see how their positions reflect the typical form of the different positions that Christians in Latin America today assume towards revolution and violence. The purpose of this anthology of texts or dossier is in fact none other than to illustrate the positions that have been briefly mentioned in this introduction.

An organized and armed struggle to give power to the popular masses—this is the position of those who have lost the illusion that profound reforms can be achieved without power effectively passing from the class that is now holding it to the class of the poor and the exploited; naturally, this immediately arouses the reaction of the present holders of power and therefore leads to violence; what is the meaning of this for a Christian, and can a Christian be violent in these cases? There are two rather significant texts: the one by Camilo Torres has long since become a classic and goes a long way towards explaining his choice in favor of armed guerrilla warfare; the other is more recent and is in the form of a declaration made by four Catholic priests at the Havana Cultural Congress in January 1968. This Congress, attended by some four hundred intellectuals from seventy different countries, analyzed the phenomenon of imperialism in its cultural dimensions: blockage of brains, destruction of national cultures, ideological justifications of domination, pressure through mass media, expansion of the American way of life as a model of life, etc. As a result of this analysis an attempt was made to propose measures suitable for opposing this phenomenon. It is very interesting to note that in his closing speech at the Congress Fidel Castro openly commended the declaration made by the four priests and went as far as developing it further.

CAMILO TORRES: MESSAGE TO CHRISTIANS

Camilo Torres is a Christian: he is reproached with having decided in favor of a radical and violent change of the situation through the assumption of power by the popular classes; he thus justifies his choice in one of his messages, the one addressed to Christians, where he says:

The essential thing in Catholicism is love towards one's neighbor: "Who loves his neighbor fulfills the law" (Romans 13:8). If this love is to be true, it must try to be effective. If beneficence, alms, a few free schools, a few plans for the construction of dwellings, in short everything that has been called "charity," does not arrive at giving food to the greater part of the hungry, nor at dressing the majority of those who are naked, nor at teaching the multitudes who know nothing at all, then we must seek effective means to ensure the well-being of this majority.

It is therefore necessary to take power from the hands of the privileged minorities and give it to the majority of the poor. This, if it is done rapidly, is the essential of a revolution. The revolution may be peaceful if the minorities do not oppose a violent resistance. Revolution is therefore the way of obtaining a government that will give food to the hungry and will carry out the works of charity and love, and this not only in an occasional and transitory manner, not only towards some, but towards the majority of our neighbors. For this reason revolution is not only permitted, but indeed becomes obligatory for Christians who see it

159

as the only ample and effective means of realizing their love for humanity.

I have abandoned the duties and the privileges of the clergy, but I have not ceased to be a priest. I believe that I have dedicated myself to the revolution for love of my neighbor. I have ceased to celebrate Mass in order to realize this love of my neighbor at the temporal, social and economic level. When my neighbor will no longer have anything against me, when the revolution will have been achieved, I shall again celebrate Mass, if God will grant me so to do. I thus believe to be observing Christ's commandment: "If then thou shalt be presenting thy offering at the altar and shalt remember that thy brother hath something against thee, leave thy offering in front of the altar and first make thy peace with thy brother, then return and present thy offering" (Matt. 5:23-24).

. . . The Christians, the Catholics, seem to be historical spectators of a world to which they are extraneous. They do not compromise themselves in the struggle. They believe that the word "world" in the phrase "My Kingdom is not of this world" has the meaning of "present life" rather than "life of sin" as it is in practice. They forget Christ's prayer to the Father: "I ask not that thou shalt separate them from the world, but preserve them from evil." Many times we separate ourselves from the world and do not preserve ourselves from evil.

. . . I have felt Christianity as a life centered on love of one's neighbor. I realized that it was worthwhile to engage oneself in this love, in this life; I thus made myself a priest in order to become a "full-time" servant of neighborly love. And it is for the same reason that I realized that in Colombia it was not possible to give effect to this love for one's neighbor by simple beneficence, but that one had to change the economic, social and political structure of the country; and then I saw that love for my neighbor was leading me to revolution. In order not to come into conflict with ecclesiastic discipline I have asked to be dispensed from this discipline, but I consider myself to be a priest for eternity. I think that I am fulfilling my ministry by struggling for the revolution and for the well-being of the majority of my compa-

160

triots. I give the name of revolution to a rapid and radical change of the economic, political and social structures. I believe that the first aim of revolution must be the taking of power by the popular class; the revolutionary achievements will stem from this: they consist principally of a real agrarian reform, a reform of the towns, the complete planning of the economy, the creation of relationships with all countries of the world, the nationalization of many means of production.

All power is today in the hands of a minority of fifty families and I do not believe that any decision in favor of the good of the majority will ever come from this minority. It is not possible for the results of the revolution in Colombia to be worse than the present situation; if one considers that countless children die of starvation every day, if one considers that girls at twelve years of age are given to prostitution, if one considers that thirty thousand peasants have died on account of the injustice of the system, then this revolution cannot be worse than the present situation.

We have launched a watchword that says that we are the friends of all who are revolutionaries and the enemies of all who are counter-revolutionaries. I can truly collaborate with the communists, because I think that the Communists are revolutionaries. Above all, we shall have to face up to the problem of the United States, because the Colombian bourgeoisie is closely tied to North American interests. Thus, just as they have invaded the Dominican Republic, I think that the United States has already decided to intervene not only where there will be communist governments, but wherever there will be governments contrary to North American interests, as the United States government has already stated. Nevertheless, I believe that when the people in Colombia and elsewhere in South America will have decided to see the struggle through to the end, there will be no material power capable of overcoming a people that desires its liberty.

In Colombia there are many guerrilla fighters, and there are also some bandits: but one must distinguish between them. Guerrilla warfare is conducted by people who have political consciousness. If one has the support of the guerrilla fighters to defend oneself, to enable one to conquer the city, I think that one also has a starting point for the moment in which there will be a national revolution of the popular type, truly unitarian and organized. I am convinced that we must first try every peaceful means; but I am also convinced that the means do not depend on the popular class. I believe that the people must take power in one way or another, because the people constitutes the majority and has a right to power. It all depends on the way in which the oligarchy decides to forego its power. If it will choose a peaceful way, the people will assume power in a peaceful manner; but if the bourgeoisie does not want to surrender power and chooses to struggle violently, then the people will respond with violence, because I believe that the people have sufficient justification for a violent struggle.

Camilo Torres returns to his choice for a violent revolution in the sense of a radical change in the power situation in another text published in June 1965; whereas in his Message to Christians he justified violent revolutionary intervention on the basis of a socio-political analysis of his country (a goodly part of which can be applied to the whole of Latin America), he now deals in greater detail with his particular situation as a priest, and discusses it both from a theological point of view and within the context of the life of his people; here, too, Camilo makes his choice for the violent manner not only on the basis of a diagnosis that he considers to be objective, but also as the outcome of a reflection on the fundamental sense of the Christian life. From this point of view the thought of Camilo Torres represents one of the first contributions towards a "theology of revolution" and in a certain sense summarizes the position of all Latin Americans who as Christians accept the violent solution of the serious problems of their continent.

"When there are circumstances," says Camilo, "that prevent men from giving themselves to Christ, it becomes the priest's function to combat these circumstances even at the price of not being able to celebrate the eucharistic rite, which cannot be comprehended without the engagement of the Christians. . . . The priesthood does not just consist of the celebration of the rites. The Mass, which is the final objective of pastoral action, is a fundamentally communitarian action. But the sacrifice cannot be offered in an authentic manner if one has not first realized the precept of loving one's neighbor in an effective manner.

"I have been chosen by Christ to be a priest in eternity, moved as I was by the desire to dedicate myself full-time to loving my neighbor. As a sociologist I wanted this love to become effective thanks to technique and science. Analyzing Colombian society, I realized the need for a revolution in order to be able to give food to the hungry, dress the naked and ensure the well-being of the majority of the members of my people. I believe that the revolutionary struggle is a Christian and a priestly struggle. In the concrete circumstances of my people it is only through this struggle that we shall be able to achieve the love that men must give to their neighbors."

Camilo then returns to this concept of love, observing that although the Eucharist remains the supreme culmination of a Christian's dedication to and union with God, it nevertheless becomes ". . . an affront to Christ himself if the Eucharist is not the culmination of one's preoccupation, respect and love for man. Does a true Christian preoccupation correspond to the social contrasts in our country? I do not think so. What then must I do as a priest? Limit myself to sermons that will cause me to be accused of being unbalanced and a fellow traveller of the Communists the more I criticize the existing situation with a precise analysis? . . . The eucharistic sacrifice is not an individual, but rather a communal offering, and the priest offers it the more authentically when there is love in the community. If those who offer are not united by love, there must be no offering to God. Consequently, if the laymen do not dedicate themselves to the struggle for the well-being of their brethren, the ministry tends to become ritual, individual and superficial. The priest is obliged to substitute for the laymen's temporal engagement, whenever this is called for by the love of one's neighbor. When this love ceases to be considered as the patrimony of the Church, one has to give an incisive testimony of the fact that charity is the unitarian basis of the Christian community. Unfortunately the testimony of the laymen does not yet identify itself in public opinion with the testimony of the Church. In this case the priest must give the testimony, the while he educates public opinion and shows it that the testimony of each of the baptized is the testimony of the Church. To see a priest get mixed up in political struggles and abandon the outer trappings of his priesthood is something repugnant to our traditional mentality. Nevertheless, I firmly believe that reasons of loving one's neighbor and of bearing witness can exist that will be sacerdotal and which will drive one into this engagement in order to obey one's conscience and, above all, to obey God."

Camilo Torres is admired even by those who do not share his justification and his choices, although they may share his acute analyses. He seems to propose his choice as the only alternative, and tries to prove it by basing himself on the great and fundamental concepts of the Christian faith; but, as is readily seen, his choice is not by any means of a "confessional" or, even better, of a "proselytizing" type; in fact, he aims at interest, dedication and love for men, and he graces these attitudes from within with a Christian animation and justification. In this sense the attitude of Camilo Torres may be understood not as unique and exclusive, but rather as one of the possible approaches open to the Christian towards revolution and radical social changes; in the case of Dom Helder Camara we shall see that this bishop, in spite of making the same diagnosis as Camilo Torres, in spite of being convinced of the need for a true "revolution" and not just a simple reform, in spite of admiring Camilo Torres and Che Guevara, still opts for nonviolence.

DECLARATION OF THE FOUR CATHOLIC PRIESTS AT HAVANA

Cuba to all intents and purposes is the first free territory in the whole of South America, having detached itself from the zone of political and economic influence of the United States; at the same time the Cuban experience is particularly interesting on account of the position assumed with regard to the socialist blocs. A number of congresses have been held at Havana that have been particularly representative of Cuba's situation and the function that it can perform within the ambit of the revolutionary movements of other countries. The Cultural Congress in January 1968 was attended by four Catholic priests; the press had spoken of them as "clandestine" priests who had not even revealed their names; they did not hide their identity, in fact they did sign their declaration; the misunderstanding may well have arisen from the fact that Fidel Castro quoted the whole text of their declaration in his closing speech, but for reasons of delicacy and reserve did not mention their names. The four priests are Mons. German Guzman (Colombia), Paul Blanquart (France), Alberto de Escurdia (Mexico) and Carlo Zarraroni (Uruguay). Their short declaration is very rich in motives that cause some groups to choose revolutionary struggle; some of these re-evoke the ideas of Camilo Torres, others show signs of a rethinking of the relationships between Christianity and Marxism. A particularly impressive element is the attack made on the United States type of imperialism; in this connection one has to bear in mind what the influence of the United States represents for a revolutionary, and also how it is generally judged by sociologists specialized in the study of the Third World (see A. P. Lentin's contribution to this volume). The declaration therefore appears as the conclusion in an operative sense of the positions previously assumed by Camilo Torres, and these, after due decantation and further elaboration, duly reappear in the very precise position taken up by these four priests. We would point out once again that we have only chosen this text because it is a particularly clear example of the attitude of the sector of Christians we are considering at the moment.

We, Catholic priests and delegates at the Havana Cultural Congress, are convinced that at the present time, and particularly in the Third World, imperialism constitutes a factor of dehumanization that destroys the foundation of human dignity, that it offends against cultural freedom and that it prevents the authentic forms of human development, promoting increasingly acute and oppressive situations of underdevelopment; that, in

165

spite of the differences existing between Marxism and Christianity with regard to the interpretation of man and the world, Marxism nevertheless develops the most exact scientific analysis of the imperialist reality and proposes the most effective stimuli to the revolutionary action of the masses; that the Christian faith implies love translated into effective service to the benefit of all man and every man; that the priest Camilo Torres Restrepo, by his death for the revolutionary cause, has given the supreme example of the Christian intellectual engaged by the side of the people; and we pledge ourselves to the anti-imperialist revolutionary struggle right down to its ultimate consequences in order to achieve the liberation of the whole man and of all men. We therefore condemn the cultural and economic blockade that American imperialism has imposed upon the Republic of Cuba, first free territory in America; we condemn the war that the United States is waging against Vietnam as imperialism's most monstrous attempt against the liberty of a people situated in the area of the Third World; and we reject every form of colonialism as a fruit of alienating and dehumanizing imperialism."

Fidel Castro read the whole of this declaration at the closing of the congress, saying that it was one of the most notable things that had happened. He then went on to comment on the phenomenon of the diffusion of revolutionary ideas that penetrate even into religious environments and observed with a certain sense of humor: "In these days I have read many communiques issued by one of the numerous Yankee news agencies that spoke of this movement, and expressed preoccupation at the development of such a (revolutionary) movement among the Catholic clergy in Latin America. They say that this movement is linked with Cuba, etc., and even accuse the Apostolic Nunzio in Cuba and a Canadian Archbishop who had come to Cuba to consecrate the new nunzio as bishop." Basing himself on the important fact of the declaration made by the Catholic priests, Fidel Castro then developed the idea that Marxism must not become fossilized in its concepts, but must face up to new facts and recent phenomena: "Nothing—he said—is more anti-Marxist than dogma, there is nothing more anti-Marxist than the petrification of ideas; and some of the ideas that are brandished in the name of Marxism seem real fossils. . . . Marxism is in need of development, it must overcome a condition of ankylosis, must interpret present-day realities in an objective and scientific manner, it must behave like a revolutionary force and not like a pseudo-revolutionary Church. These are the paradoxes of history. When we see a part of the clergy become a revolutionary force, can we resign ourselves to sectors of Marxism becoming ecclesiastic forces? I hope that I shall neither be excommunicated nor dragged before a tribunal of the Inquisition for having made these statements; but we must certainly meditate and we shall have to act in a more dialectic, that is to say, in a more revolutionary sense."

Fidel Castro's position, equidistant from and critical of both socialist blocs, offers several motives for reflection in connection with the declaration made by the Catholic priests and, more generally, in relation to the attitude of those Christians who are engaged in revolution in the sense of an armed struggle, particularly in the form of guerrilla warfare; while on the other hand one respects their choice and agrees with their diagnosis, one would not like to see the dogmatism with which Castro reproaches traditional Marxism (and, what is more, at the suggestion of new revolutionary forces that come from the very sector that is traditionally among the most anti-revolutionary) now become the dogmatism of Christians who want to impose their particular interpretation of Christian engagement in human liberation upon all.

DOM HELDER CAMARA: WHY I AM A REVOLUTIONARY, BUT A NONVIOLENT ONE

Armed violence is not the only choice. Side by side with the Christians who on the basis of their analysis of the situation of underdevelopment and oppression choose the solution of violent rebellion, there are those who do not consider this solution to be either the only one, or even the most logical one. They follow the others in their analysis, agree with the diagnosis, and have the same acute feeling that one cannot wait much longer and that nothing can be expected from timid and partial reforms; but they then opine that other means must be used in order to obtain what the local and national oligarchies have not hitherto wanted to put into effect. The lucid and courageous position of this sector of Christians is well represented by the Archbishop of Recife, Dom Helder Camara Pessoa, who has become famous on account of his full engagement as a bishop in the nonviolent struggle for radical changes in his country and Latin America in general; naturally, in spite of his declared nonviolence, he is periodically accused of being a communist; a Brazilian archbishop has even accused him of being a communist activist who has slowly penetrated into the Church up to the point of becoming archbishop, so as to be able to destroy it from within! Dom Helder replies to these accusations with his customary meekness: "If repeating every day that there are hundreds of thousands of our brothers who die of starvation, that children pass away as a result of malnutrition, that people live in incredible conditions, if this means being a communist and a revolutionary, very well then, that's what I am."

Dom Helder's position reflects that of many other Christians both in Latin America and elsewhere; it is excellently summarized by a talk given in Paris of April 25, 1968 by Dom Helder himself, and which we here reproduce on the basis of his own notes and the recording that was made at the time, because Dom Helder improvised some comments of particular interest.

"It is true," said Dom Helder, "that there has been violence at all times. Today it is possibly more imposing than ever before. It is to be found everywhere, omnipresent and in many forms: brutal, open, subtle, insidious, sneaking, blind, rationalized, scientific, consolidated, anonymous, abstract, irresponsible. It is much easier to speak of violence when it is a case of condemning it from afar without possibility of appeal, and without sufficiently distinguishing its aspects and without going into the details of its hard and lamentable causes; or when one stirs it up from just as far, when one has the vocation of an armchair Che Guevara. . . . But it is a very difficult thing to speak of violence when one lives in the midst of it, when one sees that some of the most generous and capable of our fellows are tempted by violence or have already been conquered by it. I shall gladly accept your objections, your points of view, your suggestions. But I would ask you to have the patience to listen for a moment to the thought of one who not only lives in a continent with a pre-revolutionary climate, but who, while not having the right to fail in his obligations toward the Latin American masses, does not feel he has the right to sin against the light and against love.

"1) Here is a first fundamental observation needed for a good understanding of the problem of violence: the world stands in need of a structural revolution. This truth seems self-evident in the underdeveloped world. If we observe the underdeveloped world from an economic, scientific, political, social or religious point of view, we shall immediately understand that a summary, superficial revision will not be sufficient. We have to face up to a revision in depth, a profound and rapid change; we are not afraid of the word: one has to arrive at a structural revolution. Paul VI has said:

Listen well: the present situation must be faced up to with courage and the injustices that it comports must be fought and won. Development requires audacious and profoundly innovating transformations. Urgent reforms must be undertaken without delay. Everyone must generally play his part.

"Who does not know that from the economic point of view there is internal colonialism in the underdeveloped countries? In other words, that there exists a small group of privileged people in the country itself, whose riches are preserved at the expense of the poverty of millions of their fellow citizens? This is still a semi-feudal regime: an appearance of patriarchial life, but in reality an absence of the rights of the person, an infra-human situation and a true slavery. The rural workers, who are pariahs in the real sense of the word, have no access at all to the very large part of the land that the great land owners keep uncultivated in order to appreciate its value at the right moment.

"When such a situation presents itself in a continent like Latin America, entirely Christian (at least in name and in tradition), it is possible to measure the enormous responsibility that

169

Christianity has for this situation. Without denying the great examples of dedication, sacrifice, and even heroism, one has to recognize that in the past (and there is danger that this may also be true for the present) we Latin American Christians have been seriously responsible for the situation of injustice that exists in our continent. We accepted the slavery of the Indians and the Africans. And today, can it be said that we have spoken with sufficient clarity and force to the landed proprietors, to the great, the powerful? Or do we close our eyes and help them to preserve a good conscience once they have covered frightening injustices with their alms destined for the construction of churches (often scandalously big and rich, in acute contrast with the misery that surrounds them) or with alms for our social works? Have we perhaps not proved Marx to have been right when he showed to the pariahs a passive Christianity, alienated and alienating, a true opium of the masses?

"And yet, Christianity is full of the need for justice and brotherhood. Christianity is still here with its message of eternal redemption. Because our love for man is animated from within by a Love that exceeds the dimensions of this world and brings a radically new element to it. For this reason Christianity is also the format of an integral development, and this includes economic development; because the Scriptures teach that God wanted man in his image and likeness, that he gave him domination over nature to complete the creation. If we Latin American Christians accept our responsibility for the underdevelopment of our continent, we must help to promote the profound changes in the field of social life, and particularly in politics and education. Politics must not remain the property of the privileged who prevent basic reform, distort it or leave it on paper. Education is so far from the needs of an ever growing technology that we can well understand the discomfort of the students who deride the university reforms they have to suffer, reforms that are superficial, weak and without any audacity.

"What I am saying about Latin America can readily be applied to the whole of the underdeveloped world: there is urgent need for a structural revolution. It is less easy to understand that even the developed world stands in need of a structural revolution. But is its very development not a proof of success? Why then think about a structural revolution? But let us reflect for a moment about the two most valid expressions of development, one which has taken place in the capitalist regime and the other in the socialist regime: the United States and the Soviet Union.

"The United States is a living demonstration of the internal contradictions of the capitalist regime: it has succeeded in creating underdeveloped sectors in the midst of the richest country in the world (about 30 million North Americans live in conditions that are unworthy of the human kind); it has succeeded in arousing the fratricidal strife between white and black; under the pretext of anti-communism, but in actual practice for thirst of prestige and expansion in zones of influence, it is now conducting the most shameful war the world has ever known. The dominant system in the United States is so irrational in its rationality that it succeeds in creating a unidimensional existence, a robot existence, and which leads the young people of many different cultural traditions to feel themselves called upon to construct a juster and more human society creating a new social context in order to humanize technology.

"Soviet Russia, for its own part, feels itself to be solely guided by scientific humanism because it is inspired by Marxism. In practice, under the pretext of defending itself against capitalism, she continues to maintain an iron curtain and a wall of shame; she does not succeed in admitting a pluralism within the ambit of the socialist world; Soviet Russia and China behave toward each other just like two capitalist powers; and Marxism is considered to be an untouchable dogma. Marx did not succeed in making a distinction between the essense of Christianity and the weakness of Christians who in practice have too often reduced it to an opium for the people. But now there is a profound change; today, in practice as in theory, an attempt is being made to live a Christianity, and also to make it be a Christianity that is anything other than an alienated or alienating force, but which incarnates itself in humanity, just like Christ. And Soviet Russia does not yet succeed in understanding this.

171

"At New Delhi both Soviet Russia and the United States have once again shown an equal lack of comprehension and an equally bad will vis-à-vis the Third World. All Asia united at Bangkok, all Africa united at Algiers, all Latin America at Tequendama and the whole of the underdeveloped world in its letter drafter at Algiers continues to say in vain that the problem of the relations between the countries of abundance and the countries of poverty is not a question of aid, but rather of justice on a world scale. But the two super powers, supreme incarnations of capitalism and socialism, remain blind and deaf, closed and blocked by their egoism.

"How can one avoid the developed world outstripping the underdeveloped world by an ever-growing margin? Eighty-five percent of mankind, and tomorrow it could easily be 90%, lives in misery in order to make possible the super comfort of the remaining 15%, and tomorrow only 10%. At this point, who can still refuse to admit the ineluctable need for a structural revolution in the developed world?

"2) At the moment of asking ourselves whether the structural revolution of which the world stands in need must necessarily presuppose violence, we should note that violence already exists and is already being used, at times even unknown by those who denounce it as the scourge of society. It exists in the underdeveloped world; the masses in infra-human conditions are being subjected to violence by small groups of privileged people, by the powerful. We know that when the masses want to become a people and make an effort at basic education or popular culture, when they organize themselves into trade unions or cooperatives, their leaders are labelled as subversives and communists. Of them it is said: 'They show themselves to be rebels against established order; they must be outlawed, they must disappear so that order may reign.' This is the order of disorder!

"When it comes to 'law,' this is too often an instrument of violence against the least strong, or it just reduces itself to some beautiful phrases in the text of the declarations, as the one about the fundamental rights of man, of which the world is now celebrating the twentieth anniversary. A good way of celebrating this anniversary would be for the United States to ascertain whether any one of these rights is really being respected in two thirds of the world.

"But violence also exists in the developed world, in the capitalist sector just as in the socialist one. In this connection there are some signs of restlessness that speak very clearly. There are Negroes that pass from nonviolence to violence; the Negro apostle of nonviolence falls, spreading enormous sadness; a tremor of horror shakes us when we see on the one side young North Americans who are obliged to "over-kill" in order to safeguard the free world (but we know the real reason very well!), and on the other side young Negroes, almost boys, who are obliged to kill in order to defend their lives, or better, their half lives. At the same time we see the rebellion of the young people in Federal Germany, in Italy, in Spain, in Poland; and we must also ask ourselves the true significance of the singular protest of the hippies.

"The armaments race continues; how great would be the glory of our times if we knew that the heroes of cosmonautics were carrying out their exploits for something other than war or political and military prestige! The whole world noted how ill at ease Soviet Russia found herself when faced by the new Czechoslovakia and how she sharpened the ideological struggle against capitalism under the pretext of safeguarding the unity of the socialist bloc. The Europe of the Common Market aims at figuring among the future post-industrial societies and tries to deny that it is already losing control of its own markets in favor of the North American techno-structure. Is there any need for other flashes about the world today? Sterling, once so solid, has had to be devalued, and the old queen of the seas will perhaps be forced to abandon her splendid isolation and become integrated with the continent. The dollar is the cause of great preoccupations for our dear Uncle Sam, and this in spite of the fact that his economic situation is always strong. Even the shadow of peace succeeds in bringing restlessness to thousands of workers who live by war and eat through death. Not even automation has a tranquilizing influence and mass unemployment remains a nightmare in highly industrialized countries where one would have said that the retraining of workers presented no problem. The national and international trusts are already stronger than the strongest states, and they arrive as far as making it impossible to capture the killers they have sent to eliminate certain personalities that were beginning to become a little too troublesome. One may well say that these trusts are the true rulers of the earth, and that they maneuver revolutions and wars. You yourselves may easily enlarge the list of what I have called "signs of restlessness," but which are also signs of violence, more or less camouflaged, both in the capitalist world and in the socialist one. There can be even less doubt as regards the violence the developed world is using against the underdeveloped world, as I have recalled in connection with the second UNCTAD Conference. When faced by this triple violence (i.e. within the underdeveloped countries, within the developed countries, and by the latter against the underdeveloped countries), we can well understand why people think, talk and act in terms of liberating violence, redeeming violence.

"If the powerful in the underdeveloped world do not have the courage to forego their privileges and to grant justice to millions of people in infra-human situations; if governments introduce reforms that remain on paper, how can one put a brake on the young who are tempted by the radicalism of violence? How much longer will it be possible to put a brake on the young people in both parts of the developed world, young people who are the launching platform of the agitation of tomorrow, if the signs of restlessness and violence continue to multiply? How much longer will the atomic bombs be more powerful than the tomb of misery that is coming into being in the Third World?

"3) May I now be granted the humble courage to take a position. I respect those who in conscience feel bound to opt for violence, not the all-too-easy violence of the armchair guerrilla fighters, but those who have proved their sincerity by sacrificing their lives. I feel that the memory of Camilo Torres and Che Guevara merits as much respect as that of Martin Luther King.

"But I accuse the real instigators of violence, all those who from left or right offend against justice and prevent peace. My personal vocation is that of a pilgrim of peace, following the example of Paul VI: personally I would prefer a thousand times to be killed rather than kill. I hold that this personal position is based on the Gospels. An entire life of efforts made to understand and live the Gospels has led me to the profound conviction that the Gospels, if they can and indeed must be called revolutionary, are so in the sense that they require a conversion from each one of us. We do not have the right to close ourselves in egoism; we must open ourselves to the love of God and the love of men. It is enough to think of the Beatitudes, the essence of the evangelical message, to discover that the choice for Christians is clear: we Christians are in favor of nonviolence which is not by any means a choice of weakness and passivity. Nonviolence means believing in the force of truth, of justice, of love, more than in the force of wars, killings and hate.

"If this may sound rather like moralism to you, please be patient for another moment. If the option for nonviolence is rooted in the Gospels, it also has a foundation in reality. Would you like to hear some realism? In that case I shall make you note this: if an explosion of violence should break out in any corner of the world, but particularly in Latin America, you may be sure that the great ones, the super powers, will arrive immediately, even without a declaration of war, they will be there and we shall have a new Vietnam. Do you want some more realism? For the very reason that we must arrive at a structural revolution it is quite indispensable that we should first promote a "cultural revolution," but in a new sense. For the simple reason that if mentalities do not change in depth, the structural reforms, the basic reforms will also remain on paper and will remain ineffective.

"I address myself particularly to the young people. I put the following question to the young people of the underdeveloped countries: what is the use of achieving power if you do not yet have models suited to your countries, made to measure as it were? Up to now they have taught you models that may well be valid, but valid for developed countries. While we continue to exert an ever more courageous moral pressure on those who are responsible for the situation that exists among us, you should try to prepare yourselves for the responsibilities that will undoubtedly weigh upon you tomorrow; try now to help the masses to become a people. You know very well that material and physical underdevelopment presupposes intellectual, moral and spiritual underdevelopment or brings it in its wake. To the young people of the developed countries, be they capitalist or socialist, I want to say this: rather than thinking about going to the Third World to stir up violence, remain where you are to help make your countries of abundance conscious of the fact that they too stand in need of a cultural revolution that will introduce a new scale of values, a new vision of the world, a global strategy of development, the revolution of man.

"And now a final observation. I have just been to Berlin, a guest at the World Congress of International Catholic Youth. The sight of this divided city made me ask myself this: how can Europe accept the laceration of Berlin in its heart, the symbol of numerous lacerations throughout the world? How can humanity allow itself to be divided and torn between East and West, and even more seriously between North and South? Only men who can achieve inner unity within themselves will be valid instruments of the miracle of being violent like the prophets, true like Christ, revolutionary like the Gospels, but without offending against love."

Latin America Between Rhetoric and Violence

The poor have the right to defend themselves against organized violence. The position of Dom Helder is significant and represents the position not only of many Christians in the Third World, but also the position of many bishops. But it is criticized by other Christians and by other bishops; these hold the view that the responsibility of judging the effectiveness of an armed defence against "institutionalized violence" at any given historical moment must be left to individuals and political movements; these Christians are characterized by their clear and decisive denunciation of this violence of the rich, and also by their justification of the right of the poor to defend themselves against it, even if armed struggle should be the only effective means of doing this.

There are some extremely indicative texts relating to this position. First of all, there is Hubert Lepargneur; after the voyage of Paul VI to Bogota he sums up the Latin American situation, which moves between rhetoric and violence, and criticizes the possibilities of the Movement of Liberating Moral Pressure launched by Dom Helder on July 19, 1968. The Bishop of Crateus, A. B. Fragoso, one of the youngest and most dynamic of the Brazilian bishops, defending himself against the accusations moved against him in public opinion on account of his having mentioned the Cuban experience as being an example for the Latin American countries, offers a lucid and impressive picture of the most immediate local reality, the one that is decisive in pushing certain people towards precise choices. This is followed by two letters: the first is written by some Latin American workers to Paul VI, the other by eight hundred Latin American priests is addressed to the bishops meeting at Medellin. The documents are of an exemplary spontaneity and clarity, and their lucid passion characterizes the consciousness that is being born in ever wider circles of the Third World.

HUBERT LEPARGNEUR

"In Colombia Paul VI has given expression to some heartfelt appeals to encourage the Latin American governments to undertake the structural reforms on which the beginning of social justice in this continent depends. With the courtesy and the humor that distinguishes them, the ruling classes of Latin America can do no other than reply:

We willingly take note of these appeals. Or rather, they fully correspond to our own most profound aspirations, so much so that we have already nominated special commissions everywhere to study these problems. The dossiers are accumulating year by year, translating our desire to throw light upon all the implications of the situation. No efforts will be spared in this investigation. We have thus forestalled the appeals of Your Holiness in this sacred struggle we are conducting in defence of the Christian civilization that is our pride.

"We would be wrong to want to contradict them; these owner classes have very serious preoccupations to face; let's mention two of them:

"1) What shall they do with all the money they are gathering in their private accounts, fruit of the lands from which they would never have expected such fertility? A problem that becomes all the more serious when one thinks of the rapid devaluation of the currency in these countries. Raoul Presbish, a noteworthy witness by virtue of his position, notes that 5% of the population in Latin America enjoys an income that is 15 times greater than the earnings of the rest of the population. As they cannot spend all their money in Latin America and desire to enjoy the advantages of the developed countries they transfer a good part of their capital which thus becomes lost for the purpose of the development of the country in which it came into being. Some five billion dollars have left Latin America in this way between 1946 and 1962.

"2) How can they avoid a popular and social revolution modifying the structures that permit them to preserve their traditional privileges? One certainly cannot ask the Church to pronounce herself in favor of the maintenance of the status quo of misery. One can only ask her to lend her help, the support of her moral authority, side by side with the armed forces, in a Christian and anti-Marxist society to avoid and condemn violent revolution. All the rest is the affair of the governments and the owner classes; no profound transformation is possible without their consent, and they know just where to go. The capitalist aristocracy therefore essentially asks two things of the Church: a) a condemnation in principle of misery and injustice, strong and decisive, so as to bring votes in favor of reform; b) an unconditional condemnation of violence. In this case they are thinking only of bloody violence, without ever meditating on the fact that the need that still today condemns more than half of the children in northwest Brazil to die before reaching the age of five years is no longer a necessity of a bio-physical order (unless it be an instrumental one), but rather a necessity in the order of the socio-political structures. Social morality has not yet become conscious of the changing significance of phenomena that are surely of long standing.

"It is implicitly understood that the first request made upon the Church remains a platonic one; otherwise it would presuppose a voluntary foregoing, at least in part, of the anachronistic privileges of the owners and the rulers, and history has hardly accustomed us to imagining this as possible. The second request can be executed immediately and unconditionally, even though in doing so one forgets the moral norms of legitimate defence. Does not man therefore have a natural right to defend himself to the extent of using force against an unjust aggressor who threatens his survival and that of his family? The Movement for Liberating Moral Pressure, launched by Dom Helder at Rio de Janeiro on July 19, 1968, originates from intentions to which one cannot but pay homage; but this movement of nonviolence that aims at exercising a decisive pressure on the structures unfortunately completely lacks the conditions of effectiveness that would permit it even partially to attain its purpose. These are the application of three articles of the Declaration of the Universal Rights of Man of 1948: Article 3 on the right to life, liberty and personal security; Article 4 against every form of slavery and serfdom; Article 23 on the right to work. Even in this formulation the movement has obtained the support of only a quarter of the Brazilian bishops (four bishops have given their adhesion). The first "pressures" consist of the celebration of October 2, 1968 (centenary of the birth of Gandhi) and November 2 (All Souls' Day, with particular emphasis on the memory of the martyrs of liberty). Any practice that is legal in present-day Brazil is absolutely inoffensive as far as the structures of the regime are concerned; any effective pressure is normally considered illegal and is therefore excluded from a program under the patronage of bishops.

"The Pope had hardly left Colombia (the only country in continental Latin America to have a concordat and thus to be officially a Catholic country) after having opened the CELAM assembly, when the Brazilian government, trampling underfoot every judiciary legality regarding the processes of expelling foreigners, decided to expel from its territory Pierre Vauthier, a

French priest from the community of Saints Peter and Paul near São Paolo. A worker priest, Vauthier has never been militant in political terms, but took part in a strike at the Osasco factory where he worked. The case merits examination: the simple fact of having demonstrated his solidarity with the poor in the injustice that is done to them (bearing in mind the Declaration of the Rights of Man signed by Brazil in 1948; without mentioning the natural right so frequently invoked in matters of conjugal morality) has led to Father Vauthier being expelled from a very Christian country, where the government claims to be leading "the greatest Catholic nation on earth." But how, then, does the hierarchy conceive its work, its function? What practical execution does it intend to give to its noble intentions of high moral inspiration that have caused the Pope to receive the tribute of almost unanimous applause?

"What we here in Latin America, among many other things, see every day as laden with consequences is precisely this: the hierarchical Church has not seen or understood, unless it simply omits to draw the consequences, that charity today, just like injustice, passes through the almost invisible and anonymous social structures, often shrouded in a luxurious decorum and a refined courtesy that have laws of their own. The tears of a starving child or the blood of a wounded man move one far more than the cold consideration of impersonal structures; but these go much further, both as regards the instauration of a more fraternal world and for destroying men. More than the simple faithful to whom the preaching is directed, in the last resort it is the Church that cannot serve two masters.

The Appeal of Eight Hundred Latin American Priests

In July 1968 the Assembly General of the CELAM (Latin American Episcopal Committee) met at Medellin in Colombia; one of the principal subjects was to be that of development, the Christian engagement in this process, and inevitably the problem of revolution also reared its head; the basic documents to be discussed were published shortly before the opening of the assembly. There was little time to reach many people in the immense Latin American continent; nevertheless, a group of priests succeeded in making contact with about eight hundred priests (400 Argentine priests, more than 200 Brazilian ones, 100 Uruguayans, 50 Bolivians, and a few from other countries) for the purpose of submitting a text to be presented to the assembly. The text represents the position of a growing number of Latin American priests and Christians. Particularly noteworthy, apart from the sociological analysis, is the component reflecting the pastoral preoccupation of the priests, not in a scheme of paternalism and proselytism, but in the consciousness of giving a loyal service to the human needs of their brothers.

Priests of various Latin American countries, worried by the situation in which the majority of the population of Latin America finds itself and the position of our Church in this situation, we turn with filial respect towards the pastors of our continent. It is our desire to present our apprehensions to them and to make them aware of our worries. "The violence of the Latin American continent" is being talked about with growing insistence. Some are beginning to be preoccupied. Some are afraid. We want to face up to it as pastors of the People of God and as ministers of the Gospel of Love who try to interpret "the signs of the times."

In this perspective we feel obliged to inform our bishops and possibly the world of the fundamental result of our pastoral reflection: Latin America has been a continent of violence for several centuries past. This is the case of a violence that a minority of privileged has exercised ever since the colonial period against the immense majority of an exploited people. It is the violence of hunger, of abnegation, of underdevelopment; the violence of persecution, oppression and ignorance; the violence of organized prostitution, of illegal but effective slavery, of social, intellectual and economic discrimination. Latin America at present is a continent of violence, because in it there exist large regions in which the average of the daily calories per inhabitant oscillates between 1,500 and 2,000, while the normal quota required for the development of human life lies between 2,800 and

181

3,000 calories per day. Large regions in which more than 70% of the children present symptoms of malnutrition, with all the physical, psychic and intellectual consequences that this implies.

Reality is no less irritating with regard to the economic situation of Latin America, particularly when one compares it with that of other regions. "The degree of economic development can in part be measured by the average level of incomes which barely reaches 300 dollars per annum, without forgetting the great differences between the various Latin American countries and between the various social groups of each individual country. This income is equivalent to a third of the average European income and a seventh of the North American one. The rhythm of economic growth is so slow that the level of European incomes will only be reached in 45 years" (see the preliminary base document for the second general conference of the Latin American episcopate, page 4).

This same violence manifests itself in the educational, habitational, political, and even the religious order. "Latin America shows us a population with almost 50% illiterates, without counting the functional illiterates among the adult populations" (base document, page 7). The marginal urban population . . . "forms entire quarters at the periphery of the city constructed with refuse materials, where the low level of life, the lack of hygiene, the crowding and the dimensions of the hovels forces this population to live in inhuman conditions." "Others live crammed into old houses in the old part of the city" (base document, page 5). In Latin America . . . "one lives a democracy that is more formal than real, in which at certain times there lacks an authentic liberty of organization. The political systems are characterized by various forms of oligarchy. . . . In many countries the military group constitutes a powerful pressure force that is determinant in politics" (base document, page 10). "The Church has been infected by the hypertrophy of the political powers. Where it is an official religion, its religious hands are identified with the political power. In other parts they are tied to the dominant classes and to the powerful. The Church has at times kept silent in the face of abuses of civil and military power. . . ." (base

182

document, page 10). We call this "violence" because it is not a case of the fatal and inevitable consequences of a technically insoluble problem, but the unjust fruit of a situation that is deliberately maintained.

We become ever more convinced that the cause of the enormous human problems from which the Latin American continent is suffering is fundamentally rooted in the political, economic and social system that reigns in almost all our countries—a system based on "gain as the essential driving force of economic progress, competition as the supreme law of the economy, private property of the means of production as an absolute right," denounced by Paul VI in *Populorum Progressio*. This is the system that each year bleeds the national budget of our countries, setting aside enormous sums for useless military expenditures in defence of the interests of privileged minorities, while our people continue to be immersed in hunger, ignorance and isolation because "there are no means" for creating industries and constructing schools and roads. This is the system that permits the sweeping advance of "international money imperialism" (*Populorum Progressio*) which, either stealthily or openly, introduces itself into our countries and prevents an authentic continental development—an imperialism that becomes daily more powerful through the use of our cheap labor, installing its industries in our countries, and sucking our natural riches when it "buys cheap raw materials in Latin America and then sells the finished products needed for development at ever higher prices" (base document, page 5). This is the same imperialism that then seeks to deceive our people by making appear as a "benevolent" loan what is really nothing other than a way of "negotiating" on the international plane. All this is nothing other than a pale sketch of the centuries-old panorama of the state of violence caused by the structures of national and international economic, political, social and cultural power that seek to dominate our people.

For some time past, however, a new element has appeared in this panorama of misery and injustice. This is the fact of the rapidly awakening consciousness of an exploited people that

183

senses and notes the real possibilities of its liberation. For many people this liberation is not possible without a fundamental change of the socio-economic structures of our continent. There are quite a few who consider that all the possibilities of succeeding in this by exclusively peaceful means have already been exhausted. In view of the means of repression used by the privileged minorities to prevent this process of liberation there are now many people who see no other solution than the use of force on the part of the people.

This conclusion is also being reached by many militant Christians who sincerely reflect their life by the light of the Gospels. We, ministers of the Gospel of Jesus Christ, placed by our mission in the midst of this people who proclaim the Word of Truth and of Justice, feel obliged to interpret this panorama in the light of the Christian revelation. This light permits us to see clearly that one cannot condemn an oppressed people that finds itself obliged to use force for its liberation without committing a grave injustice against it. If this condemnation were to come from the Latin American Church, the Church would once again appear as "the opium of the people" in the service of those who for centuries have practiced the violence of exploitation and oppression, causing hunger, ignorance and misery.

On the other hand it would be impossible to understand a Church that contradicts itself by condemning the violence of those who today want to free themselves from the oppression of an unjust system, while it pays homage to the heroes of a political independence that was not exactly conquered by nonviolent means. We are of the opinion that it is not the task of the ecclesiastic hierarchy as such to determine the technical forms that constitute the most effective and objective solution of a problem of a temporal order. Neither is it its task to prevent men, be they Christians or otherwise, from seeking such a solution with an ample margin of liberty in accordance with the evangelical principles of fraternity and justice. We believe that it is not even the task of the hierarchy as such to proclaim the concrete form of a radical change in human structures. We believe, however, that the prophetic denunciation of situations of injustice that make a change necessary forms part of its specific mission. On the other hand, failure to oppose the violence of the oppressors would be equivalent to indirectly provoking the legitimate violence of the oppressed.

These facts and reflections lead us confidently to ask the following of our pastors united in assembly:

1) That in considering the problem of violence in Latin America they should by every possible means avoid equating or confusing the unjust violence of the oppressors who maintain this "ill-starred system" with the just violence of the oppressed who find themselves obliged to have recourse to force in order to obtain their liberation.

2) That they should denounce with absolute clarity and without ambiguity the state of violence with which the powerful, be they persons, groups or nations, have for centuries kept the people of our continent in subjection; that they should proclaim the right of these people to legitimate defence.

3) That they should clearly and firmly exhort the Christians of the continent to opt for everything that contributes to a real liberation of Latin American man and to the instauration of a more just and fraternal society in close collaboration with all men of good will.

4) That they should grant these Christians an ample margin of liberty in the choice of the means they consider most suitable for obtaining this liberation and constructing this society.

With this we do not seek to constitute ourselves as standard bearers of an indiscriminate violence. On the contrary, we are anguished and deplore the thought that one must accept the fact of the use of force to re-establish justice. In spite of this, we are driven by necessity to accept the responsibility that the present hour requires of us. This is not even a case of idealizing violence, but rather of giving a new dimension to the repeatedly recognized principle that an unjustly oppressed community has the right to react, and even to react violently, against an unjust aggressor. The aggression we are denouncing is that of the oppressive structures that prevent the integral and harmonious development of a large part of our populations and silently, but effectively, resist any form of "audacious and profoundly rennovating transformation" (*Populorum Progressio*). In the hope of being harkened and of having contributed to the work in which you are engaged we greet you with filial respect in Our Lord.

Antonio Battista Fragoso:
The Courage of Tiny Cuba

Dom Antonio Battista Fragoso was one of the best-known assistants of the JOC (Young Catholic Workers) in northeast Brazil, when at a very early age he was nominated Auxiliary Bishop of Sao Luca, the ancient city founded by the French when they tried to install themselves in Brazil in the 17th century. In 1946 he was sent as resident bishop to the diocese of Crateus, a small town barely known to Brazilians themselves, situated in the huge province of Ceara. It was a poor township, surrounded by even poorer villages, a diocese that counted six or seven priests at the time of Dom Fragoso's arrival; a rural population dispersed over the large estates, in the margins of any form of political life, deprived of the essential services, abandoned to its fate or to the arbitrage of a political and economic power that the population itself could do absolutely nothing to control. In these conditions the presence of a bishop has always been a blessing; he knows how to deal with the rich and obtain a little money to found schools, construct hospitals or nurseries; he can obtain the necessary funds from ministers when he wants to provide some social service; the banks do not refuse him the means if he proposes to create some kind of cooperative; and he can also have contacts with the international Catholic assistance agencies.

Dom Fragoso came to Crateus with the intention of putting an end to this stereotype of the bishop as impressario, administrator, "constructor of civilization." He systematically refused to be the intermediary between the few rich and his flock of poor, between the government, always generous when it is a case of approving a project presented by a bishop, and the citizens whose most urgent needs are habitually destined to official oblivion. Instead of seeking money to assist the poor, Dom Fragoso set himself the task of teaching them to organize themselves so as to

186

become capable of giving weight to their claims and rights; instead of distributing easy alms to be found among the rich and the powerful, he set out to give them a human education and to instill into them a personal consciousness and the pride of men and the sons of God. In this sense Dom Fragoso is less "politicized" than Dom Helder, the more so as he finds himself in a very different situation; but the force of his type of work is incisive and positive to the point that this young bishop lost in the wilds of Ceara soon came to arouse very strong reactions that were dominated by the fundamental fear of many environments: the awakening consciousness of the popular and peasant masses, and therefore the creation of true centers of uprising and, above all, of reasoned and lucid claims that will no longer accept paternalistic intervention, however generous it may be.

Dom Fragoso's contribution to this volume was written on an occasion when he had made a statement about Cuba in which he had expressed a judgment that was very different from the one that is normally accepted in the leading political and ecclesiastical circles of Latin America; at the same time he takes the opportunity of developing his thought as regards the general Latin American problem. This is what Dom Fragoso has to say:

1) In the city of Natal there is a newspaper called *El Poty*. A journalist from this paper came to see me to ask my opinion about the Church and the problems of today, youth, Latin America, the danger of America becoming "cubanized," the priesthood and celibacy, birth control and the Church. Among the two hundred odd lines of my statement there was one in which I said: "The courage of tiny Cuba could be a symbol and an appeal for the liberation of Latin America." That same evening a professor of law at Natal, Mr. Paolo Bezerra, who belongs to the DOPS (Editor's note: Department of Political and Social Order, i.e. the political police), sent a telegram to the papers and the Archbishop to say that the Catholic conscience of the state had been disturbed by the statement of the Bishop of Crateus. That same evening the students of the faculty of law, finding an echo of their preoccupations in the phrase I had used, displayed my interview in a highly visible position in the faculty. The

same evening a judge from the interior of the country arrived from far away to congratulate me and to express his solidarity, because "it is essential that there be an element of honesty at least in the person of a bishop; the honesty of recognizing what is true even in those who do not think like ourselves." The same evening the press correspondents sent a cable to Rio de Janeiro, not to quote my interview or my complete thought, but just that small, isolated phrase. They did not say "the courage of tiny Cuba," but said "Cuba, an example for Latin America, declares the Bishop of Crateus." The same evening the Rio de Janeiro television service spread the news, but mutilated my thought.

The next day the *Jornal do Comercio* at Recife published a leading article that took a position against my statement. Two days later *O Diario de Pernambuco* published the statement made by the "usineiros" (sugar mill owners) of the State of Pernambuco, who in a telegram to the Minister of Justice had protested against the speech made by the Bishop of Crateus. . . . The *Correiro de Ceara* spread the following headline over five columns: "The Usineiros of Pernambuco protest against the Bishop of Crateus." I thought it to be my duty to give a personal explanation, not to the papers or to the authors of the articles that have appeared in the various papers, but to the people who had not understood what I thought, but had heard only a mutilated phrase . . . On the other hand I must explain myself to many people who have asked me for clarifications about my thought.

2) You have every right to require me to speak clearly. Why did the Bishop of Crateus say that the courage of tiny Cuba was a symbol and an appeal for Latin America? There are various replies that I can give. The first: In Cuba there was a shameful dictatorship, the dictatorship of Fulgencio Batista. General Batista was dictator for thirty years and dominated Cuba. More than half the wealth of the island was in the hands of the Batista family. Eighty percent of the Cubans were illiterate. Only the privileged had access to the universities, the land was divided into scandalous states. Each weekend the rich North Americans came to make the rounds of this "underworld" and to spend their

time in Cuba's cabarets. Who protested against this dictatorship that assassinated 23,000 political prisoners? A young Catholic university student by the name of Fidel Castro felt in conscience bound to protest. But to protest in the public square, as one tries to do here, would have been sufficient for him to be shot, just as 23,000 political prisoners were shot without trial. He therefore went to protest as a guerrilla fighter in the Sierra Maestra. He was joined by Father Sardinhas; he was joined by a bishop; he was joined by several other priests and leaders of the Cuban JOC; he was joined by numerous militants of Catholic Action in Cuba, because everybody thought that to liberate the island from the abominable and immoral dictatorship of General Fulgencio Batista was a sacred cause. This is where the story begins.

After having won and established the revolution, Fidel Castro said: "Let's get on with the agrarian reform." The agrarian reform that the Brazilian peasants desire and of which they stand in need, and which the government has not had the courage to carry out. Fidel Castro drafted the text of a law and Mons. Serentes, Archbishop of Santiago, said in a pastoral letter that the agrarian reform called for by Fidel Castro was inspired by the social doctrine of the Church. But the agrarian reform involved the sugar cane lands. Ninety percent of Cuba's budget depends on sugar cane, and this was being sold exclusively to the United States. Forty percent of the land under sugar cane cultivation was in the hands of North Americans tied to the Department of State. When Fidel Castro wanted to apply the agrarian reform to the 40% of the land belonging to North Americans, these latter protested and the State Department said: "There will be no reform here." In the name of a small island of six million inhabitants Fidel Castro now said to the richest and best armed giant in the whole world with all its two hundred million inhabitants: "We shall not give in! The reform will be carried through!" He did not have to wait long for the reaction of the United States: "In that case we shall no longer buy your sugar"; and as 90% of Cuba's economic life blood came from sugar, this meant suffocating the small island with its six million inhabitants. At this point Russia said: "In that case we shall buy your sugar; we will give you money and send you our technicians." And thus Fidel Castro and Cuba passed into the orbit of the U.S.S.R. and the popular socialist republics. Whose fault was it? I don't have to answer that question. The answer comes from a famous name, John Kennedy, who had this to say in his electoral campaign: "The mistake, the responsibility for Cuba leaving the unity of the continent and entering into the Soviet orbit weighs upon the shoulders of the United States who failed to give their support to the aspirations, the liberty of the small island." We must not therefore throw the blame on Fidel Castro.

Immediately afterward Fidel Castro mobilized the entire country. He said: "Eighty percent of the Cubans are illiterate. If the people are illiterate they will always remain in the margins of society. It is essential that all adult citizens of Cuba should become conscious and participate in the struggle for the liberation of their country." He then closed the universities and the secondary schools. He assembled the teachers, trained them, and in three months the adult Cubans became literate. A beautiful gesture on the lines of the Gospels, a gesture that we have failed to make in Brazil, that we did not want to make. Here in our State of Ceara we still have our 70% of illiterates. Why doesn't our government have the courage to act as Fidel Castro did?

3) Recognizing these evangelical virtues of a man who today is no longer a Christian—that is being a Christian. To hide them would be a betrayal of Christianity. If one does not have the courage, if one does not have the honesty to see what is good in one's own enemies, then one is no longer a Christian. The fact that the Bishop of Crateus can give testimony of an elementary honesty in speaking of Cuba is equivalent to recognizing the positive things to be found in his people. . . . The other evening I paid a visit that has been very useful to me: a visit of fraternal dialogue. I went to see General Dilermano to explain to him what I am saying at this moment. I said to him: General, why doesn't the Brazilian government close the universities and the secondary schools, why doesn't it prepare a million Brazilians, teachers, on the basis of the method of Paul Freyre, so as to render the illiterate adult peasants conscious within four months?

(Editor's note: Paul Freyre's method associates literacy with awakening consciousness, because it makes the adult students participate in the organization of collective life. Paul Freyre had to leave Brazil after the military coup d'etat in 1964.) They will then organize themselves and carry out the social reforms. The liberation of the people will not be effected either by the government, or the rich, or the powerful. The peasants will liberate themselves by uniting their efforts. They must not be led by the nose either by bishops, or by President Costa e Silva, or by the Brazilian army. They must not be pushed around by those who retain economic power, who enrich themselves at the price of common love and who send their sons and daughters to study in the big cities, never to return to engage themselves with the people of their region.

We are only taking the first steps. If at the moment of taking the first steps such a lot of ado is made about a little phrase said by the poor Bishop of Crateus, what is likely to happen later? And later I would like to be able to count upon you and all the others. We have done nothing other than take the first steps. The peasants remain in the margins of society. Our government does not respect the peasants. It is preparing a charter for the peasants at Brasilia, without consulting the thousands of workers who are already in the trade unions. The trade union dues are being collected by agents who deceive the people by saying that they are sent by the Bishop of Crateus to exact these dues. The trade union dues are being collected by agents who in the name of IBRA (Brazilian Institute for Agricultural Reform) want to politically organize improvised trade unions from one day to another, so that the politicians will be able to maneuver them as they please. Brothers, in other sectors of the country we still have not made the first steps. And even here we have done nothing but the first steps. But afterwards, who will liberate the peasants? The peasants have not yet woken up. There is a small group, certainly. But, my friends, it is essential to wake up all the others.

The typical position of Dom Fragoso, which represents that

of a vast area of opinion, is particularly clear in his statement to General Dilermano: "The peasants will liberate themselves. . . . They must not be led by the nose either by bishops, or by President Costa e Silva, or by the army." It is essential that they be "woken up." For this reason Dom Fragoso has seen Cuba as an example for the whole of Latin America; not as an example, as he himself says, for Marxist-Leninist education, but rather for the awakening of the consciousness of a people through education, through respect for the feelings, the needs, the views of millions of Latin American campesinos and workers.

A LETTER FROM LATIN AMERICAN WORKERS TO PAUL VI

The Confederacion Latinoamericana Sindical Cristiana, in the name of its five million members, sent this letter to the Pope before he began his voyage to Bogota. The letter is very long and it is not possible to reproduce it completely in this volume; we shall therefore try to give the most significant passages directly concerning the problem we are considering, i.e., examples of the position of vast groups of Christians to which this section is dedicated.

Brother Paul, we have read your letter entitled *Populorum Progressio,* addressed to all men the world over. This letter of yours displeased quite a few people in Latin America. In particular, it definitely disgusted the dominant groups who are privileged minorities but who manage Latin America as if it were a fief or an estate. These groups have even called you a "communist," a "subversive," just as they have applied these names to us and to other Latin Americans who want the full development of our people. More elegantly, but also more hypocritically, there are others who have said that you have served up some "warmed-up Marxism," that your letter "has no possibility of being immediately applied in Latin America." Cardinal Cardijn once said that if the Pope came to Latin America he would immediately be arrested as a communist. . . . We do not think they will arrest you this time when you come to Colombia. You are in fact going to a country where the Church has great power, because it has systematically identified itself with the powerful and the opulent. For this reason the armed forces and the police will be there to "guard you" and not to arrest you as a "subversive" or a "communist." . . . However, you must not allow yourself to be deceived. These same armed forces are used in Colombia, just as in the whole of Latin America, for the purpose of stopping and liquidating all the movements and activities of the workers and the peasants. . . . Now, the label "communist" is no longer fashionable. Communism, for reasons of its policy of world hegemony, has transformed itself into an excessively conservative and conformist ideology. Therefore, the term that has now become fashionable is that of "subversive"; nowadays this is more real and dangerous for the dominant groups. Thus, anybody who simply protests or objects, anybody who works for a little more justice, liberty and dignity, is immediately labelled as a "subversive" and is persecuted, imprisoned, tortured, and in many cases he must abandon his country and his family. We are well aware of what happened to your diplomatic representative in Brazil. The military government denounced him as a "subversive" for the simple fact that he sympathized with some bishops and priests in this country who support the revolutionary efforts of those who want the full development of this Brazil, so great, so exploited and so oppressed. If this happens to the prelates of your Church, try to imagine what happens to the poor who have nothing behind them other than their misery and their intense human hope to free themselves once and for all from this misery.

But let us return to your letter about the development of peoples. There has not only been the disappointment and the aversion of the rich and powerful. Your letter greatly pleased the workers, the peasants, the women who work, the inhabitants of the city peripheries, and the youth of the people. You seem very great in your mission as the advocate of the poor. Your language resembles our own, and it can be understood by all. It is clear and direct, it is hard like our suffering in denouncing the century-old insensitivity of the possessors of the riches and the power. It seems very worried about the increasingly insecure destiny of our peoples and the poorer and less favored classes who form the overwhelming majority of our continent. For this reason we have desired to address you as "Brother Paul" in our letter, because this is how we see you and feel you, our brother in a common and collective destiny. You have interpreted our daily anguish of men who form part of the "people who today appeal to the opulent peoples with dramatic accents."

You have placed yourself on the side of those who are tormented by hunger, by the lack of culture, by infirmity. You have put your finger on the sore of our frustrated hopes, our invariably forgotten yearnings, our rebellions almost always suffocated even before they occur by the oppression of the powerful and the opulent. . . . But, Brother Paul, note that religion and the Church in Latin America have continually been used to justify and consolidate the injustices, the oppressions, the repressions, the exploitation, the persecution, the assassination of the poor. . . .

The letter supplicates Paul VI to be very careful during his voyage in Latin America not to become instrumentalized by political, financial, intellectual, cultural and ecclesiastic forces that will attempt to use his presence to serve as a screen for all the abuses and privileges; Paul VI should take up a clear and decided position in favor of the poor. The letter then continues and directly introduces the subject of violence and revolution:

Do not think that we are defending the guerrilla fighters. We know that this is not the road for Latin America, for the moment. But you must not forget that independence and political liberty in the history of our continent were conquered on the basis of simultaneous guerrilla warfare in all our countries. And nobody in Latin America can yet foretell the "final arguments" to overcome situations that cry vengeance to the heavens and which constitute "true tyrannies." . . . And, Brother Paul, we speak of revolution because this is what we have at heart and what the Latin American reality demands. It is impossible to give precedence to human promotion and the integral development of our people without pronouncing oneself on the political means that condition them. For this reason the exigencies of the conscience of each Latin American and the urge for love and solidarity in

194

the heart of each authentic Christian pass through the undelayable need for effecting this social revolution. It is not right to associate this indispensable revolutionary process in Latin America with violence as a system or with hate for its own sake. This revolution is born out of a profound desire for justice, dignity, liberty and love for man. When we compare the values that must be realized and the objectives that must be attained with the concrete situations to be found in our countries, we clearly see that revolution is the only road. What you say in your letter with regard to the development of the people and what must be done and attained, and what we ourselves think should be done and attained, make us note an enormous difference when we compare it with the actual situation, with what should be done and what is really done. We must conclude that there is a lot to change in our society. But the distances are enormous and these changes must therefore be profound. And when we see that this situation cannot and must not last much longer, because nobody can ask patience and resignation of millions of human beings who have not even the most elementary things to enable them to exercise their right to live, we must also conclude that these changes must be effected rapidly without just continuing in hope, as you yourself say in your letter.

It is certain that this process of profound and rapid changes cannot be improvised, but must be planned and carefully prepared if it is to be effective down to its last consequences. And when we find ourselves faced with these changes of the economic, political, social, cultural and even religious structures that must be effected in our continent and, what is more, changes that must be profound and radical, carried out with a rapid and intense rhythm, one cannot doubt that Latin America is clearly proposing a revolutionary process with all its consequences. You yourself say this in your encyclical, when you assert "that development requires audacious and profoundly innovating transformations. Urgent reforms must be undertaken now." We are essentially saying the same thing, even though you use different words. But we are agreed on the fact that Latin America needs a social revolution as a first step towards creating the objective and

195

subjective conditions for a full development of our people and for a definite liberation and promotion of Latin American man. . . .

You say in your letter that a revolutionary process can be justified when "an evident and prolonged tyranny seriously offends against the fundamental rights of the person and dangerously damages the common good of the country." We cannot generalize; that is as dangerous in Latin America as it is in any other country; but one does not have to know a great deal to realize that there are situations in many countries that constitute true economic and political tyrannies; tyrannies of national oligarchies; tyrannies of the armed forces that settle everything by force of arms; tyrannies of international money imperialism. And in many of our countries these tyrannies have already lasted for more than a hundred years; they offend the fundamental rights of the majority of Latin Americans; and they take no account at all of the common good of their countries. If the common good is the good of all and particularly the good of the poor who constitute the majority of our country, then, Brother Paul, we must tell you that this common good does not exist and has never existed in Latin America.

Even with your own arguments we can and must justify the need for social revolution in Latin America. And be very careful, Brother Paul, because there are many privileged, rich and powerful who are hoping that in Latin America you will speak against this revolutionary process, and will rather invite the Latin Americans to enter into a process of "gradual and peaceful evolution." You should know that those who hunger and thirst for justice and for bread, the poor, speak of revolution in Latin America; but those who are sated with power and riches speak of "gradual and peaceful evolution," that "due time must be allowed for all things," that "one must have patience." We must thank God that in Latin America there are priests and bishops who have understood the significance of a "Church of the poor" and who speak today with increasing strength and clarity of the need for carrying out a profound social revolution.

And we hope that you will not tell us how we must make

the revolution, because this lies within the competence of our responsibility and our initiative. But we hope, as in a new Pentecost, that you will invest us with the fire of the Spirit and of love, that you will uplift and animate us, that you will give us your grace and your blessing so that we may face with audacity, with rapidity and without loss of time the gigantic and profoundly Christian task of redeeming the poor, the men, the peoples of Latin America from every misery and oppression. . . .

When one speaks of revolution the problem of hate and violence immediately comes to the forefront. But we must not even speak of hate. We do not believe in hate, but in love and human solidarity. And the motive of the revolution is nothing other than love and human solidarity. Hate is counter-revolutionary. But the problem of violence still remains open. We think that in Latin America this point is being exaggerated. Some try to create a theology of violence, others a theology of nonviolence. As if the important aspect of the revolution were violence or nonviolence, forgetting that if a revolution is to triumph, what must be done is simply to carry the revolution through to its ultimate consequences. There can be no doubt, Brother Paul, that violence established as a system and understood as a repression of reason and spirit by means of brute and physical force cannot and must not today constitute the effective road for the social revolution in Latin America. There is a profound and rich humanist tradition in our continent that would reject the use of violence as a system. But, Brother Paul, we have an anguished and valid question. Do you think that the rich and the powerful who today manage Latin America as a personal fief, just as they did a hundred years ago, will surrender their positions, their incomes, their privileges, by virtue of a peaceful process, by virtue of civic, moral and spiritual conviction? Experience has taught us that little or nothing can be hoped from possible "conversions" of the rich, the opulent and the powerful. The poor know that they must count more on themselves and their own strength than on the help of the rich. There may be some exceptions; but they are very rare, and limited to a few people. It would be an illusion to hope passively for a free conversion of those of whom the Patriarch Abraham says in the scriptures: "The rich will not listen even to one who has risen from the dead." . . .

Each change in favor of the people, each process of popular promotion, each attempt for greater justice and liberty has always been repressed in Latin America by the violence of the established order which has never failed to use all the forms of violence to prevent justice and liberty from being achieved. For this reason, Brother Paul, we only want to be sincere and realistic. In Latin America it is impossible to carry out any social revolution without overcoming every type of resistance on the part of the privileged. This is inevitable and does not depend on the will of those who sincerely desire a profound social revolution. And in order that God and history may judge what will happen in this Latin America of ours, you should know that the violence of those who want to make a humanist revolution will not exist except in relation to the resistance of those who are opposed to the request of the Latin American peoples, who simply ask to regain their dignity. And this is the reality of violence. It does not exist in the heart of those who want to make the revolution, but it exists in the heart of those who oppose it for egoism and for the interests of small groups. . . .

As can clearly be seen, the letter of these workers and trade unionists makes the same diagnosis and the same proposal for a radical structural revolution that we have noted elsewhere, for example in Dom Helder or even in the groups that are closer to the ideals of Camilo Torres. It is very interesting to note how the letter very clearly turns the relationship between revolution and violence upside down; violence is not the violent gesture of the guerrilla fighter, but is the century-old situation in which the dominant classes want to maintain the existing structure of Latin American society; the "violence of the poor" is always something minute when compared to the repression by the oligarchies; this may seem to be innocuous, benevolent, bloodless, it may even become colored by paternalism and veined with Christian and humanitarian sentiments; but ever wider sections of the popular masses are becoming conscious of having a full right to demand a concrete break in the established order (or disorder).

At this point the dominant groups intervene with the legal means they retain to strangle this explosion of consciousness, which is the true and profound revolution: the Brazilian facts of December 1968 (just a few months after the passionate appeals made by Paul VI to the groups responsible for wielding power in Latin America!) do nothing other than demonstrate the complete correctness of the diagnosis and the forecasts made by these workers in their letter to the Pope prior to his voyage. Another point to be stressed is this: one must not even speak of hate and violence; a structural revolution by itself does not need it, quite the contrary—hate is counter-revolutionary (this is very different from the conception of the class struggle based on the hate between social classes); but if violence should break out, it is nothing other than the reply to the sneaking declarations of good will and the requests for patience that the established political and economic powers have by now been putting forward for centuries. And the central point of the letter, which characterizes the position represented by these workers, is the request that the Pope "should not tell us how to make the revolution, because this lies within our competence and our initiative." It is the problem of the liberty of the operative choices.

THE CHRISTIAN MUST NOT USE VIOLENCE

The discourse on revolution is necessarily connected with the one about violence; anyone who intends to face up to the Latin American situation and who refuses the idea of a simple and slow revolution, because this would correspond to a continuous increase in the well-being of the rich and a further impoverishment of the oppressed classes, accepts the idea of the structural revolution; this revolution is understood as a rapid and radical change of complex situations and systems. But whereas almost all the more advanced Christians in Latin America accept this idea, not all of them accept the perspective of violence to obtain a radical change not granted by the dominant classes; they insist on saying that violence is anti-Christian and anti-evangelical, even when it is a case of facing up to institutionalized

199

violence. People holding these views normally have recourse to the encyclical *Populorum Progressio* and the speeches made by Paul VI at Bogota in August 1968; apart from the reference to the evangelical doctrine, it is also observed that institutionalized violence is always a lesser evil than the violence of revolutionary movements. The problem is really rather more complex, but in this context the accent tends to be put on the legality of the use of violence, and the problem thus risks becoming a little artificial and casuistic; however, even those who reject every form of violence do not always reject the need for a revolutionary action. The rejection of every form of violence is principally expressed at the level of the magisterium, but naturally this formulation also represents the personal position of many Christians.

From the *"Pacem in Terris"* to Bogota

In his encyclical *Pacem in Terris,* John XXIII had already expressed his opposition to violence and violent revolution (No. 162 of the encyclical); nevertheless, the same encyclical cited a text from Thomas Aquinas' *Summa theologica*: "Human law has the character of law for as long as it corresponds to just reason; from this it appears that it takes its force from eternal law. But to the extent to which it departs from reason, it no longer conforms to the notion of law and is rather a form of violence" (*Summa* I-II, Q.93 A3 and 2).

The encyclical *Populorum Progressio* took this theme up again in 1967, and although it again rejected the violent forms, it nevertheless admitted in a brief passage that there might be some cases where every other attempt to achieve a true evolution had failed; even the analysis of the limit situations was not avoided and was carried out with clarity, admitting the evidence of sociological diagnosis as regards the underdeveloped sectors; at this point the problem of violence immediately presented itself and was treated in Nos. 30 and 31 of the encyclical:

There are certain situations where injustice cries out to the heavens. When entire populations, deprived of essentials, live in a state of dependence such as to keep them from any form of initiative and responsibility, and also from every possibility of cultural promotion and participation in social and political life, there is a great temptation to reject such injuries to human dignity by means of violence. And yet we know: revolutionary insurrection—except in the case where an evident and prolonged tyranny offends seriously against the fundamental rights of the person and dangerously harms the common good of the country —is the source of new injustices, introduces new disequilibria, and provokes further ruin. One cannot combat a real evil at the price of a greater evil.

Having excluded recourse to violence, the encyclical nevertheless goes on to say that "the present situation must be faced with courage and the injustices that it comports must be fought and won. Development requires audacious and profoundly innovating transformations."

This second statement and the open diagnosis of the present Latin American situation were amply taken up again by Paul VI at Bogota in the course of his voyage in August 1968. At the same time, however, he returned to the subject of the rejection of violence, motivating it in greater detail. Three texts are particularly indicative, and naturally were greatly expected; they were also the subject of ample discussions and of rather critical and energetic reactions. We do not here intend to make a critical reading of the pontifical statements, but merely to annotate them as indicative of the line chosen by both the pontifical magisterium and by many bishops and faithful.

FROM THE SPEECH TO THE CAMPESINOS (AUGUST 23)

Permit me finally to exhort you not to place your faith in violence or in revolution; this attitude is contrary to the Christian spirit and can also delay rather than favor the social elevation to which you legitimately aspire. Try to give better support to the initiatives in favor of your education, for example the efforts made by "Accion Cultural Popular"; try to remain united and organize yourselves under the Christian sign, to put yourselves in a position to modernize the methods of your rural work; love your fields and cherish the human, economic and civil function as workers of the soil that you exercise.

We are well aware that the Latin American realities find themselves faced with a situation of profound and truly historical crisis that involves many acute aspects of anguished preoccupation. Can the Pope ignore this ferment? Would he not have failed in one of the purposes of his voyage if he returned to Rome without having faced up to the central point of the problem that causes so much inquietude? Many, particularly among the young, insist on the need for urgently changing the social structures which, in their opinion, do not permit the attainment of effective conditions of justice for the individuals and the communities; and some conclude that the essential problem of Latin America cannot be resolved except by violence. With the same loyalty with which we recognize that similar theories and practical attitudes frequently have their ultimate motivation in the noble impulses of justice and solidarity, we must say and reaffirm that violence is neither evangelical nor Christian; and that brusque and violent changes of the structures would be fallacious, ineffective in themselves and certainly not in conformity with the dignity of the people, which requires that the needed transformations be effected from within, that is to say through an appropriate awakening of consciousness, an adequate preparation and that effective participation of all which ignorance and the conditions of life, frequently infrahuman, prevent from being achieved today.

FROM THE INAUGURATION SPEECH AT THE CELAM GENERAL ASSEMBLY (AUGUST 24)

If we must favor every honest effort for promoting the renewal and the elevation of the poor and of all those who live in conditions of human inferiority, if we cannot express solidarity with systems and structures that favor grave and oppressive disparities between the classes and the citizens of one and the same country without their being able to put into practice an effective plan for remedying the unsupportable conditions of inferiority from which a population without strength is suffering, we ourselves nevertheless repeat once again in this connection: neither hate nor violence is the force of our charity. Among the various roads towards a just social regeneration we cannot accept either that of atheist Marxism, nor that of systematic rebellion, and even less so that of bloodshed and anarchy. Let us distinguish our responsibilities from the ones of those who, unlike ourselves, turn violence into a noble ideal, a glorious heroism, a pleasing theology. To repair the errors of the past and to cure the present infirmities we must not commit new errors, because it would be against the Gospels, against the spirit of the Church, against the very interests of the people themselves, and against the happy sign of the present hour, which is that of justice on the march toward fraternity and peace.

The position assumed by Paul VI is therefore very clear. We make no mention of the criticisms that have been moved against it; instead we do note that many have accepted the full legitimacy of his position, but add that just as the Christians who choose the road of revolution cannot condemn those who reject it, the same should happen in this case; one is bound to observe, in fact, that it is not at all clear how the choice of revolution can be excluded on evangelical grounds (which would be equivalent to a theological motivation) while at the same time condemning a "theology of revolution." We are thus brought back with increasing insistence to the theme of the freedom of choice of the options of Christians in their operative political choices.

THE LATIN AMERICAN EPISCOPATE AT MEDELLIN

One thing was particularly noted in the remarks made by Paul VI on the subject of revolution: the absence of any mention of the brief passage, important as it is, contained in the *Populorum Progressio* when it refers to the case of "an evident and prolonged tyranny that seriously offends the fundamental rights of the person." Now, the almost unanimous diagnosis tends increasingly to define the general situation in Latin America as a tyranny of this type, and especially in the case of some particular situations; this silence has therefore induced an inference regarding a possible step backward from the position of the encyclical *Populorum Progressio,* and there have been quite a few rather energetic reactions. The general assembly of the CELAM would thus seem to have found itself faced with the more decided positions of the Latin American Christians and the unequivocal diagnosis of the human and social situation in Latin America on the one side, and the firm positions of Paul VI on the other; the discussions at Medellin were evidently stormy, and this not so much as regards the debate for or against violence, but rather as to whether it was logical or obligatory for the Church to accept or exclude a choice that in the last resort would seem as if it had to be left to individual Christians.

The final text of the Medellin meeting, however, was rather well balanced and avoided any specific condemnations; although referring to the statements made by Paul VI, it returned to the distinction that had previously been made in *Populorum Progressio,* and also tried to give some realistic motivations regarding the concrete good of the Latin American countries, although in the last analysis it seemed to respect the decisions made by engaged individuals or groups of Christians. The text we reproduce below is taken from the final document on "The Church in the Service of Man."

Violence constitutes one of the gravest problems that pose themselves in Latin America. One cannot abandon to the impulses of emotion or of passion a decision on which the entire future of the countries of the continent demands. We would seriously fail in a pastoral duty if in this dramatic dilemma we were not to recall to the conscience the criteria that derive from the Christian doctrine of evangelical love. Nobody will be surprised if we categorically reassert our faith in the fecundity of peace. This is our Christian ideal. "Violence is neither Christian nor evangelical." The Christian is peaceful and does not blush about it. He is not simply a pacifist, because he knows how to fight (Paul VI in his message for peace of January 1, 1968). . . . If the Christian believes in the fecundity of peace for arriving at justice, he also believes that justice is an indispensable condition for peace. One cannot ignore that Latin America in many of its parts finds itself faced with a situation of injustice that can be defined as institutionalized violence because the existing structure violates fundamental rights, a situation that requires global, audacious, urgent and profoundly renovating transformations. We must not be astonished if the "temptation of violence" comes to life in Latin America. One must not abuse the patience of a people that for years has been supporting conditions that would hardly be acceptable to those who have a better consciousness of human rights. In a situation that gravely offends against human dignity and therefore against peace, we appeal as pastors to all the members of the Christian people to assume their grave responsibilities in the promotion of peace in Latin America. We would like our appeal in the first place to reach all those who have a greater share in riches, culture or power. It is known that there are leaders in Latin America who are sensitive to the needs and try to effect remedies. These leaders themselves recognize that the privileged as a whole frequently exercise pressure on the governors with every means at their disposal and prevent the necessary changes. In some cases this resistance assumes drastic form and destroys life and goods. For this reason we make this urgent appeal to them not to take advantage of the peaceful position of the Church to oppose, either actively or passively, the profound changes that are needed. If they jealously maintain their privileges and above all if they defend them by themselves employing violent means, they will become responsible before history for provoking "the explosive revolution of despair" (Paul VI at Bogota, August 23). Equal responsibility for injustice is shared by all those who do not operate in favor of justice to the limit of their possibilities and remain passive for fear of the personal sacrifices and risks that every audacious and truly effective action implies. Justice, and therefore peace, are conquered by means of a dynamic action of arousing the consciousness of the popular sectors and organizing them so as to exert pressure on the public powers who are frequently impotent in their social projects without popular support. And lastly we appeal to those who, faced by the gravity of the injustice and the illegitimate resistance to change, place their hopes in violence. With Paul VI we recognize that their attitude often finds its ultimate motivation in the noble impulses of justice and solidarity. We are not here referring to pure verbalism that does not imply any personal responsibility and detaches itself from fecund and peaceful actions that can be carried through immediately. If it is true that revolutionary insurrection can be legitimate in the case of an evident and prolonged tyranny that seriously offends against the fundamental rights of the person and dangerously harms the common good of the country, irrespective of whether it is due to a person or to obviously unjust structures, it is also true that violence or "armed revolution" generally generates new injustices, introduces new disequilibria and provokes further ruin: one cannot combat a real evil at the price of a greater evil. If we then consider the complex of the circumstances of our country, if we take account of the Christian's preference for peace, the enormous difficulties of civil war, its logic of violence, the atrocious evils it generates, the difficulty of building up a regime of justice and liberty by starting from a process of violence, we ardently desire that the dynamics of the people to become conscious and organized should place itself in the service of justice and of peace. And lastly we want to echo the words of the Holy Father speaking to the priests and deacons of Bogota when, referring to all those who suffer, he says: "We shall then be able to understand their anguish and transform it not into anger and violence, but rather into the strong and peaceful energy of constructive works."

It seems clear that the Medellin text fully accepts the position assumed by Paul VI and much of it is taken from the encyclicals *Pacem in Terris* and *Populorum Progressio*. At the same time, however, the text is very complex and reflects several of the basic problems that agitate Latin America; in particular, the rejection of violence has a less authoritative aspect and there is an attempt at motivation ranging through a rather ample field: from the evangelical doctrine to sociological and psychological considerations, the equilibrium of forces, etc. It is evident that the magisterium cannot propose all this as religious doctrine, and it is therefore only a position that is submitted to the reflection of engaged Christians, who will then make their decision on the basis of the reflections they have made, though guided by the evangelical spirit.

The true problem in the whole of this agitated discussion on revolution and violence, in fact, concerns the significance, the limits and the direction of the Christian engagement; in the case of Medellin it has been said that one should not seek concrete directives of a political order in the declarations of the episcopate, because "the assembly is essentially religious." But this is exactly where the difficulty lies. After the Council and the encyclical *Populorum Progressio,* the "religious" can no longer be understood in an abstract and stratospheric sense, independently of engagements that concretely concern development and consequently politics. In fact, one cannot think of God from a Christian point of view independently of the integral salvation of man: body and soul, temporal and spiritual, individual and society. If the policy that dominated the medieval Church is being left further and further behind so that it shall no longer be thought that the ecclesiastic institution desires to dictate a "Christian policy," the "apolitic" position is now equally in the process of becoming outdated. No Christian can engage himself in the human city, as the Council invited him to do, without finding himself faced with options that necessarily imply a policy. If the Council has excluded a political engagement of the Church as an institution, it has nevertheless obliged every Christian freely to decide his political engagements within the framework of a substantially open pluralism.

The problem is certainly new, thorny and delicate, not least because this very apolitical position can in certain situations play in favor of a particular policy, just as a certain type of non-violence can play in favor of violence. The education traditionally received by Christians can lead them to an apolitical conception that today increasingly assumes the appearance of a weakness rather than a virtue; it is the weakness of the man who is continually suspended in the world of theory, who faces up to all the hypotheses, but who never succeeds in participating in a concrete action, even one that may not be wholly effective.

The whole problem nowadays moves within new terms that have been proposed by the new generations; we cannot risk rejecting these terms point blank merely because the solutions are far from being mature and clear. If there exist some general principles that a Christian cannot ignore, such as those expressed by Paul VI, then it is still very difficult to imagine how the plurality of engagements that Christians are supposed to be able to assume can be put into practice within the framework of these still abstract principles.

For this reason, perhaps, the positions assumed by Dom Helder, by Dom Fragoso, or by the Latin American workers who have written to Paul VI, can give us some precious indications for a more serene and realistic solution to the dilemma that is worrying Latin America, and not just Latin America alone: each Christian finds his strength of love, of justice and of liberty in the Gospels; but each Christian must choose where and how to apply this inner strength; this brings him face to face with political choices depending on human and sociological analyses that no longer fall within the direct competence either of the evangelical message or the teachings of the magisterium. In whatever form one may postulate this arduous problem, there remains the fact that while we can still discuss it in an atmosphere of relative calm, people in Latin America are forced to face it day by day; and in that situation it is no longer "tomorrow" that counts, but "today."

Chapter Ten   Violence or Nonviolence in the Transformation of Society

In our opinion, we are not here concerned with two opposed terms that have no common basis. The violence to which we refer has nothing in common with that of a delinquent attacking his victim. Likewise, the nonviolence in which we are interested is not that of a bourgeoisie comfortably installed in a country that has been conquered with more or less trouble. Violence and nonviolence here represent two different options for resolving a unique problem: the injustice that divides the world into poor and rich, into citizens living in abundance and a disinherited multitude, into free men and slaves, and in doing so cuts right across continents and nations.

When faced with the problem of unjust structures that permit the well-being of a minority at the price of sacrificing the majority, Christians, just like any other men, cannot but assume a position of opposition and condemnation. Differences only arise when they have to pronounce themselves on the strategic problem of the means.

Numerous Christians condemn the use of violence on ethical grounds and hope that justice will be established through a peaceful evolution, an adaption of society.

Others proclaim the need for a true revolution; however, at the moment of choosing the concrete means for bringing it about, and for reasons that are often very different from each other, they recoil from everything that in one way or another might imply the idea of violence, which is often identified with hate.

But there are also many for whom violence is the only solution. Only through violence—which, as they point out, is not a reality introduced into the world by the revolution, but rather a preexisting and already active factor—will the modern slaves of hunger, underdevelopment and illiteracy obtain their liberation.

In this following dossier, we have assembled a large variety of views and have arbitrarily classed them into three groups:

    I. Peaceful evolution: opposition to violence,

    II. Revolution without violence: liberating pressure,

    III. Effective revolution: violence as an instrument of libera-ation.

Numerous shadings can be inferred within these fundamental positions, and they do in fact exist. Moreover, the frontiers between any two positions are often rather subtle, almost imperceptible. One only has to invert the value and the weight of a concept and one will be faced by an entirely different vision, without this being revealed by the terms that are used. In classifying the various texts, therefore, we have not only considered the texts themselves, but also the more or less explicit tendency of the source or the authors.

I. Peaceful Evolution: Opposition to Violence

As already mentioned, we included in this group the opinions of those people who, without by any means defending the status quo, are opposed to a revolution in the real sense of the term and prefer the road of peaceful transformation and evolution, the only road, in their opinion, that accords with the evangelical message of love and with the respect due to the established order. At the base of this view one often finds a conception of civil authority of a theocratic character, a tendency to consider the function of the Christian in society in a fixed perspective, and also a ready identification of violence with the means employed for overthrowing the established order; the violence involved in maintaining this order is passed in silence.

Collective Pastoral Letter of the Chilean Bishops

The Christian is a man of peace, and peace is "the work of justice." This is "a permanent task" if society is to live in order.

210

Injustice is a disorder, and disorder can only be remedied by struggle. "Peace is not handed to us on a platter, it has to be constructed." But struggle is not violence.

A strong temptation of violence is gripping the whole of Latin America. Violence is presented as the only effective solution, its heroism and its mystique are being exalted, and this is unrealistic. Because at the bottom of this impatient violence there is more hate than love, more passion than reason, more desire to destroy the present evil than to construct the future good, and most of the time this good remains confused and far away.

We call for "fewer combatants and more workers" in Chile. Let us construct rather than destroy, let us reform what can be reformed and replace what can not, let us conserve what must be conserved, and let us do all this in a great sweep of creative audacity, but without hate, with well-defined objectives, and under the responsibility of the authorities.

In any case, we Christians have a mission of our own in this process; the love of Christ is our specific originality. Who struggles without love is not a Christian.

Let us struggle for justice, but let us struggle with love. (*Documentation Catholique,* No. 1529, December 1, 1968, col. 2090)

Pastoral Letter from Mons. Antonio M. Aguirre, Bishop of San Isidro (Argentine)

Without this equilibrium of love, every class struggle, even if it is directed towards a just end, will contribute towards embittering the relations between men, and if it is not heroically dominated by love it will only replace one oppression by another. If we cannot teach others how to transform present-day society and its flagrant errors without hate, we shall already have forsaken the essentials of the Christian message.

The struggle for justice, particularly the one that aims at liberating the working class from the oppression it is suffering, must not only be judged from the point of view of effectiveness, but also by the spirit that animates it. A struggle that will perhaps have to be hard, but upright, fair, without hate. Every Christian struggle, if it is to be Christian, must contain a ferment of love and unity that is stronger than hate.

I know very well that many people will tell me that the existing structures are so unjust and so un-Christian that one cannot eliminate them without having recourse to a violent revolution. But history shows us that at the beginning of Catholic life the situation offered very little hope to the preachers of the Gospels from a human point of view. And yet, the strength and the light of the Word of God, become preaching and witness, set the ancient world on fire and slowly but surely transformed it.

The regrettable "triumphalism," so much talked about these days, may at times take on a new form by reaction; it then becomes much more sensational and much easier to adopt extremist revolutionary positions than to carry into practice in the anonymity of everyday life the inner conversion that Jesus Christ expects from us. This conversion presupposes fidelity to the Lord and his Gospels incarnate in one's own life. To be faithful to the Divine Master and his teaching is the only means whereby we can be faithful to the men of our times and to our role in history (John 12:24-25).

At the Vatican Council II we discarded the idea of dominant authority. Let us now divest ourselves of the idea of dominant subversion! Saint Paul, in his letter to Philemon, teaches us that all of us, without any exception, are the slaves of Christ.

II. Revolution Without Violence: Liberating Pressure

Many Christians, in spite of ardently desiring the revolution and working actively to achieve it, refuse the use of violent means either on account of ethical or strategic reasons. In their own way they make use of the nonviolent techniques of opposition made famous by Gandhi in India and by Martin Luther King, Jr. in the struggle for the rights of the Negroes in the United States. Occupation, strikes with folded arms, boycotts, refusal to pay taxes, refusal to bear arms, these are some of the means they employ. The partisans of this intermediate position find themselves exposed to the attacks of the other two parties.

Their revolutionary attitude, their desire for a brusque transformation of the social order, makes them suspect to some. To others, their strategic choice, considered to be insufficient on a general level, becomes equivalent to an involuntary alliance with the defenders of the existing situation, the defenders of the "established disorder."

Helder Camara: Only One Option: Violence?

May I be granted the humble courage to take a position:—I respect those who felt in conscience bound to opt for violence, not the all-too-easy violence of the armchair guerrilla fighters, but those who have proved their sincerity by sacrificing their lives. It seems to me that the memory of Camilo Torres and Che Guevara deserves as much respect as that of Pastor Martin Luther King, Jr.

—I accuse the true instigators of violence, all those who from left or right offend against justice and prevent peace.
—My personal vocation is that of a pilgrim of peace, following the example of Paul VI; i.e., personally I would prefer a thousand times to be killed rather than kill.

This personal position is based on the Gospels. An entire life of efforts made to understand and live the Gospels has led me to the profound conviction that the Gospels, if they can and indeed must be called revolutionary, are so in the sense that they require a conversion from each one of us. We do not have the right to close ourselves in egoism; we must open ourselves to the love of God and the love of men. It is enough to think of the Beatitudes, the quintessence of the evangelical message, to discover that the choice for Christians is clear: we Christians are on the side of nonviolence, which is not by any means a choice of weakness and passivity. Nonviolence means believing in the force of truth, of justice, of love, more than in the force of wars, of killings and of hate.

If this may sound like moralism to you, please be patient for a moment.

If the option for nonviolence is rooted in the Gospels, it

also has a foundation in reality. Would you like some realism? In that case I shall say this to you: if an explosion of violence should break out in any corner of the world, but particularly in Latin America, you may be sure that the great ones will arrive immediately, even without a declaration of war, the super powers will be there and we shall have a new Vietnam. Do you want some more realism? For the very reason that we must arrive at a structural revolution it is quite indispensable that we should first promote a "cultural revolution," but in a new sense. For the simple reason that if mentalities do not change in depth, the structural reforms, the basic reforms will also remain on paper and will remain ineffective.

I now address myself particularly to the young people. I put the following question to the young people of the underdeveloped world: What is the use of achieving power if you do not yet have models suited to your countries, made to measure as it were? Up to now they have taught you models that may well be valid, but valid for developed countries. While we continue to exercise an ever more courageous moral pressure on those who are responsible for the situation that exists among us, make it your task to prepare yourselves for the responsibilities that will weigh upon us tomorrow, make it your task to help the masses to become a people. You know very well that material and physical underdevelopment brings intellectual, moral and spiritual underdevelopment in its wake.

To the young people of the developed countries—of the capitalist or the socialist regime—I say this: rather than thinking about going to the Third World and trying to stir up violence there, remain at home to help make your countries of abundance conscious of the fact that they too stand in need of a cultural revolution that will lead to a new scale of values, a new vision of the world, a global strategy of development, the revolution of man.
(*Informations Catholiques Internationales*, N. 312, May 15, 1968, p. 7)

Allocution by Cardinal Duval, Archbishop
of Algiers, to the Great Seminary of Algiers

We are presently living an hour that is full of menaces; violence is taking on an ever growing dimension and, what is even more worrisome, it is presented in ever vaster circles as the only possible means for ensuring the triumph of justice.

The truth, and one has to have the courage to say this, is that justice limits the use of violence to some very definite cases and that there is no greater outrage to justice than the generalization of violence. Pastor Martin Luther King, Jr. has written in his own blood the message to which he dedicated all his life: that justice on earth must be achieved through nonviolence.

It is certain that even when violence is legitimate—and I repeat that this is only so in very definite and limited cases—it only has a negative effect: to remove certain causes of injustice. But the whole of the positive work of justice and peace remains to be accomplished. This is a work of construction that requires lucidity, courage, patience and determination.

(April 7, 1968)

Jean Lasserre: Nonviolent Revolution?

The true problem for the Christian who wants to be faithful to the Gospels thus consists in working for the revolution, but with means that are compatible with the love of which he has to be both the witness and the instrument; above all, he must be careful not to accept violence which is a menace to life.

It is not true that we are forced to choose between capitulation in the face of injustice and armed resistance to injustice. Anybody who asserts that we are faced with this dilemma without there being another way out, thereby shows that he does not believe in Christ the Liberator.

(Ed. Sensen Verlag, Vienna, 1968)

Barbara Deming: On Revolution and Equilibrium
in Revolution, Violent and Nonviolent

If people doubt that there is power in nonviolence, I am afraid that it is due in part to the fact that those of us who believe in it have yet to find for ourselves an adequate vocabulary. The leaflets we pass out tend to speak too easily about love and truth—and suggest that we hope to move men solely by being loving and truthful. The words do describe our method in a kind of shorthand. But who can read the shorthand? It is easy enough to recommend "love." How many, even among those who like us use the word, can literally feel love for a harsh opponent—not merely pretending to while concealing from themselves their own deepest feelings? What is possible is to act toward another human being on the assumption that all men's lives are of value, that there is something about any man to be loved, whether one can feel love for him or not. It happens that, if one does act on this assumption, it gives one much greater poise in the situation. It is easy enough to speak about truth; but we had better spell out how, in battle, we rely upon the truth. It is not simply that we pay our antagonist the human courtesy of not lying to him. We insist upon telling him truths he doesn't want to hear—telling what seems to us the truth about the injustice he commits. Words are not enough here. Gandhi's term for nonviolent action was *satyagraha*—which can be translated as "clinging to the truth." What is needed is this—to cling to the truth as one sees it. And one has to cling with one's entire weight. One doesn't simply say, "I have a right to sit here," but acts out that truth—and sits here. One doesn't just say, "If we are customers in this store, it's wrong that we're never hired here," but refuses to be a customer any longer. One doesn't just say, "I don't believe in this war," but refuses to put on a uniform. One doesn't just say, "The use of napalm is atrocious," but refuses to pay for it by refusing to pay one's taxes. And so on and so on.

One brings what economic weight one has to bear, what political, social, psychological, what physical weight. There is a good deal more involved here than a moral appeal. It should be acknowledged both by those who argue against nonviolence and those who argue for it that we, too, rely upon force.
(*Liberation,* 1968, p. 6)

III. Effective Revolution: Violence as an Instrument of Liberation

The texts quoted up to now enable us to appreciate the true reasons for which the pacifists, be they revolutionaries or otherwise, are opposed to the use of violence.

The Christian thinkers who defend the use of violence do so by starting from the same concept of love. However strange this may seem, they declare that love obliges us to choose the weakest and to fight by their side in order to assure them a better and freer life. Some of them introduce a more traditional concept into Christian morality: the defence against an unjust aggressor within defined limits. In general, the defenders of violence agree with the partisans of liberating pressure as regards their dynamic and active vision of the function of Christianity within society. Almost invariably their disagreement is only of a strategic nature. Violence seems to them to be the only weapon capable of changing the existing unjust situation.

Thomas R. Melville: The Present State of the Church in Latin America

The real question is not "Whether or not the Revolution?" but rather "The Revolution: peaceful or violent?" As Christians, we cannot but desire the peaceful change, the peaceful process. Christ came to bring us peace, and man by nature wants peace for himself if not for his fellow man. But true peace is the result of justice, as the Holy Father says, and justice is the reciprocal relationship between two beings or groups where each recognizes the basic rights of the other. The revolution can only be peaceful when those who control the structures—the rich oligarchy—are willing to allow such a change to occur, recognizing the long-denied rights of the poor masses. To the degree that they oppose such a change, the masses will be forced to use ever more drastic measures, to take the power into their own hands and thus effect the change by themselves. It is the rich then, with those of allied interests, who have the real say as to whether the process will be peaceful or violent. John F. Kennedy said: "Those who

217

make pacific revolution impossible, make violent revolution inevitable."

We have only to ask then, what is the answer of the rich to the demand of the poor for their human rights? Will they allow it to be peaceful or will they oppose it with all the means at their disposal? It is only left for us now to examine the present and recent past of the Latin American power structure to see what alternative they have already picked.

Having come to the conclusion that the actual state of violence, composed of malnutrition, ignorance, sickness and hunger of the vast majority of the Guatemalan population, is the direct result of a capitalist system that makes the defenseless Indian compete against the powerful and well-armed landowner, my brother and myself decided not to be silent accomplices of the mass murder that this system generates. We began teaching the Indians that no one will defend their rights, if they do not defend themselves. If the government and oligarchy are using arms to maintain them in their position of misery, then they have the obligation to take up arms and defend their God-given right to be men.

We were accused of being Communists along with the people who listened to us, and were asked to leave the country by our religious superiors and the United States ambassador; we did so. But I say here that I am a Communist only if Christ was a Communist. I did what I did and will continue to do so because of the teachings of Christ, and not because of Marx or Lenin. And I say here, too, that we are many more than the hierarchy and the United States government think. When the fight breaks out more in the open, let the world know that we do it not for Russia, not for China, nor any other country, but for Guatemala. Our response to the present situation is not because we have read either Marx or Lenin, but because we have read the New Testament.

(CIDOC, Cuernavaca, Mexico, January 20, 1968)

Robert Cousso: The Christian and
the Struggles of Man

Another element of solution to be foreseen with some prudence is that of nonviolence. Even though this has undoubtedly made progress both in opinion and in use, one cannot see an absolute solution in it. It has so far been used in conditions that are too particular—generally conditions of impotence—for one to be able to see it as a sure and universal means, particularly in the West. One only has to take a look, even in India, at the fate of nonviolence after Gandhi, and this in spite of the presence of such an outstanding figure as Nehru, the disciple of Gandhi. The new India has taken up some very conformist positions with regards to violence and war. Moreover, a study of Gandhi's action will lead one to reinterpret its historical bearing and to put it in its proper place, however important it may be. The isolated study of Gandhi's nonviolence tends somewhat to falsify the perspectives; one has to place it within the general framework of the opposition that it aroused in India itself and add to it the other forces which, together with nonviolence, achieved India's independence. In short, nonviolence seems to be a privileged means as regards its order of values and a means that is currently gaining ground in the West, but it does not seem to be capable of replacing violence. It is just one means among others, but it is neither the only means nor, and this is even more important, an equivalent means.

("The Violence of the Poor," supplement to *Frères du monde*, No. 40-41, pp. 151-52)

Herbert Marcuse: Ethics and Revolution

The ethics of revolution, if such a thing exists, is not governed by absolute norms, but by historical ones. These do not abolish the general norms, expressions of progress towards the humanization of society.

Without entering into the problem of knowing to what extent revolutionary means can justify themselves by virtue of their possible consequences upon the freedom and the happiness of future generations, and without discussing the problem concerning the arrogation of the right to sacrifice existing privileges and freedoms, or even human lives, there really exist forms of violence and oppression that no revolutionary situation can justify, because they are a very denial of the aims of the revolution itself. Among these forms of violence one might mention unprovoked violence, cruelty and terror. One must nevertheless point out that in the course of history revolutions forge their own moral and ethical codes and that they become the source of new norms and of new general values.

In fact, the greater part of the values that are universally recognized were born in the course of revolutions: tolerance was born during the civil wars in England, the inalienable rights of man came out of the American and French Revolutions. In the beginning these ideas formed a historical force as thoughts linked to one of the parties, as the means utilized by a revolutionary movement for political purposes. Originally, violence was an element in the realization of these aims. Later these ideas acquired a significance opposed to violence, an ethical significance. In this way revolutions submit to moral norms.

The leaders of historical revolutions have never turned violence into a revolutionary value for its own sake. The contemporaries of Georges Sorel rejected his project of severing the links between violence and reason, a project by means of which he wanted to free the class struggle from all moral considerations. In comparing the violence of the class struggle in its revolutionary phase to the violence of military operations, he subordinated revolutionary violence to purely strategic calculations: the aim being the complete defeat of the enemy, violence represented a means that made it possible to attain this end. The relationship between the means and the end reduced itself to a simple technical relationship. . . .

In conclusion: the relationship between the means and the end is the ethical problem of the revolution. In a certain sense, the ends justify the means, at least when the ends clearly contribute to human progress. This legitimate end, which in fact is the only legitimate end, requires a climate that should facilitate and further its realization. The creation of such a climate may justify sacrifices, just as such sacrifices have been justified throughout history. But this relationship between the means and the ends remains a dialectical one. The end must already be visualized in the repressive means utilized for achieving it.

The sacrifices also imply violence; a nonviolent society will only become possible in a period of history that we have still to make our own.

(*Geweld en Vrijheid, politike opstellen*, Amsterdam, 1968, IDO-C Translation)

Bertrand Duclos: Let My People Go

The love of man in which we recognize our Lord has opened our eyes. On the other hand we have come to understand that there is violence and violence. We have come to understand that we cannot put the violence of oppression and the violence of liberation on the same level. The love that illumines the eyes of anyone who has chosen the Lord reveals to him that the violence of the poor is a violence that has been imposed on them, a violence that is necessary. He knows very well that the poor are the first and worst sufferers from violence, because the order of the powerful never hesitates to augment its violence when the "little ones" lift their heads. The violence of the poor is sacrificial. They spill their blood for a common liberation from injustice, for love of their fellows. It is a resistance of the spirit, an explosion of their dignity that has been left no other means for expressing itself. All ways of human expression have been closed to them, every dialogue refused, no attention has been paid to their painful and patient complaints. Nothing remains to them other than organized refusal, the deliberate will to die rather than continue living in slow motion. Only the living can die and the poor are reduced to a "half living" state.

To die in refusal, in revolt, seems like the first gesture of the rebirth of oppressed man. For him it will be the assertion of his existence, of his consciousness of being human, a consciousness that refuses to let itself be alienated by other men.

The violence of the poor is the cry of the spirit that proclaims, asserts and demands life from the bloody pulpit of men. Let us say it again, the violence of the poor is sacrificial within the most profound meaning of this term: the poor struggle for the values that make humanity and surpass their own personality.

("The Violence of the Poor," supplement to *Frères du monde*, No. 40-41, pp. 78-79)

Jalles Costa: Christians Faced
by the Problem of Violence

Let us be quite clear about one thing. I am not an apostle of violence. I should love to be able to participate in a nonviolent and effective revolution. I simply do not take my desires to be realities. My wishes do not change the situations of oppression. If there is anybody who knows where and when a true nonviolent revolution has been carried out, let him tell us about it.

I do not desire violence. Violence is imposed on me. There is no other choice. If I opt for nonviolence, I become an accomplice of oppression, I take the part of the violence of the state.

One has to make it very clear that violence is neither brutality, nor hate, nor vengeance. If I take part in a revolution that has to employ force, I have committed myself to a movement of liberation. Perhaps the mission of the Christian in the revolution is to ensure that the necessary violence will not be transformed into hate, vengeance or brutality.

Furthermore, it is a false problem to ask oneself whether or not one has the courage to kill. The essential thing is to know whether or not one has the courage to die. Sometimes the fear of killing hides the fear of dying. For a Christian this fear is a paradox. Guevara, who did not believe in eternal life, was not afraid to die. That is the reason why he is so very alive among us.

Among the temptations for the Christian there is the belief in a naive and ineffective nonviolence; solidarity, direct or indirect, with those who kill the innocents; a false hope that consists of charging God with a mission that only man can accomplish; imagining conditions that conform to his desires as a Christian. "The God who guarantees our wishes and our illusions is dead,"

writes Josef Smolik. "A theology of the death of God can become a liberation full of promise that puts us on the road towards our starving and suffering brothers in whom we encounter Christ and for whom he has prepared the future." [1]
(*Christianisme et Revolution,* Paris, 1968. Jalles Costa is a Brazilian sociologist resident in France.)

Camilo Torres: His Last Letter to the Colombians

Now the people no longer believe in anything. The people no longer believe in elections. The people know that all legal resources have been exhausted. The people know that they have no choice other than arms. The people are desperate and have decided to risk their lives so that the next generation of Colombians shall no longer live in slavery. So that the sons, for whom the fathers are prepared to give their lives today, may receive an education, a roof, nourishment, clothes and, above all, dignity.

So that future Colombians may have a country freed from North American domination.

Every sincere revolutionary realizes that the only remaining issue is the issue of arms. The people are anxiously hoping that their leaders will give the signal for battle by their example and their presence.

All Colombian patriots must put themselves on a war footing. Little by little, in all the corners of the country, experienced guerrilla leaders will come to the fore. We, too, must be ready. We must work with our closest neighbors. We must collect clothes, medicines and provisions and prepare ourselves for a long struggle.

NOTES

NOTES

Chapter 1. The Gospels and the Church as a Revolutionary Force

1. Cf. Helmut Schelsky, "Der Mensch in der wissenschaftlich-technischen Zivilisation" (Man in the Scientific-technical Civilization), "Arbeitsgemeinschaft für Forschung des Landes Nordrhein-Westfalen," *Geisteswissenschaften*, No. 96, Cologne, 1961.

2. On this subject see H. D. Wendland, "Die Macht schöpferischer Zerstörung über den Menschen in technischen Zietalter" (The Power of Creative Destruction over Man in the Technical Age), *Zeitwende/Neue Furche*, No. 6, 1966, pp. 382-90.

3. Hannah Arendt, *Über die Revolution* (About the Revolution), Munich, 1965, p. 364.

4. Ibid.

5. Paul Tillich, "Christentum and soziale Gestaltung" (Christianity and Social Structure), *Gesammelte Werke* (Collected Works), Vol. II, Stuttgart, 1962, pp. 209, 219 f. As regards the conservative parties one may consult among others O. H. von der Gablentz, *Einführung in die political Wissenschaften* (Introduction to the Political Sciences). Cologne-Opladen, 1965, p. 147 f.

6. Two works are fundamental in the very rich literature on the subject of revolution: Karl Brinkmann, *Soziologische Theorie der Revolution* (Sociological Theory of Revolution), 1948; Hannah Arendt, *Über die Revolution* (About the Revolution), 1965, possibly the most penetrating work and richest in content. The articles by Tillich and Rich mentioned in notes 8, 9 and 10 remain to this day the most interesting and profound works in theological literature on this subject. A good general introduction to the theological aspect of the problem is given by the article by E. Fahlbusch in *Evangelisches Kirchen Lexicon*, Vol. III, Göttingen, 1959, col. 639 f.

7. See H. D. Wendland, "Die Weltweit Gesellschaft und die Oekumene der Kirche" in *Einheit der Kirche?* ed. W. Marxsen, Wit-

ten, 1964, p. 74 f. Above all, see W. Schweitzer, "Christen im raschen sozialen Umbruch heute," in *Beiheft zur Oekumenischen Rundschau,* No. 2, Stuttgart, 1966.

8. Above all, in his analyses of Marxism republished in the second volume of the *Gesammelte Werke* (Collected Works): "Christentum und soziale Gestaltung," op. cit.

9. Arthur Rich, *Glaube in politischer Entscheidung* (Faith in Political Decision), Zurich, 1962, p. 96.

10. Op. cit., p. 97.

11. See the explanation and development of this notion in H. D. Wendland, "Der Begriff der verantwortlichen Gesellschaft in seiner Bedeutung für die Sozialethik der Oekumene" (The Concept of the Responsible Society in Its Significance for the Social Ethics of the Ecumenical Community), *Zeitschrift für Evangelische Ethik.* 1965, p. 1 f.

12. On this subject see the important article by P. Brunner, "Unsere Verantwortung für die Menschlichkeit der Gesellschaft und für das Recht" (Our Responsibility for the Humanity of Society and for the Law), in *Pro Ecclesia,* Vol. I, Berlin, 1966, p. 180 f.

Chapter 2. Revolution and Violence

1. *Populorum Progressio,* n. 81.

2. *The National Catholic Reporter,* February 28, 1968.

3. M. Peuchmaurd, "Esquisee pour une théologie de la révolution," *Parole et Mission,* 39, 15th October 1967, p. 635.

4. The term was recently disowned by the Pope on the occasion of the first anniversary of *Populorum Progressio* and in the course of his allocution to the cardinals on June 24, although it has been accepted by the Church and Society Department of the World Council of Churches, in its 1966 Summer meeting in Geneva. See also Arthur Rich, "La révolution, un problème théologique," in *Christianisme Social,* January/February 1967, pp. 9-16, being a report presented to the meeting of the Swiss delegates to "Church and Society" on November 24, 1966.

5. See S. Snoek, "Terceiro Mundo, Revolucao e Cristianismo," in *Concilium* (Portuguese Edition), No. 5, May 1966.

6. See Leslie Dewart, *Cristianesima e rivoluzione,* Jaca Book, 1967. "Studying the behaviour of the episcopate, and more generally that of the Cuban Church during Castro's revolution, we are bound to note how the logic of a traditional theology and a classical social doctrine have brought the Cuban bishops, priests and laymen to develop and justify what in the last analysis we might call 'a theology of counter revolution.'"

7. See "Non-violenza e rivoluzione," a round table conference

organized and published by "Sette Giorni," No. 42, March 31, 1968.

8. See *Populorum Progressio*, 30-31. This is an argument frequently resorted to by pacifists. On the occasion of the previously mentioned "Conversations on Revolution," Father Berrigan, a well-known United States pacifist, expressed the same idea when he said: "The first thing (i.e., reason for which he opposes violent revolution) would be that I believe it to be counter-productive, reactionary; I believe it creates far more problems than it solves" (*The National Catholic Reporter*, March 6, 1968).

9. See *Il Regno*, 151/2, document 22.

10. See R. Domergue, "Réflexions sur la violence," *Frères du Monde*, Supplement to No. 40/41, 1966.

11. "The absolute purpose of the state is the protection or the modification of the internal and external distribution of power; this end, in the last analysis, must seem to be devoid of sense to any universal religion of salvation. This consideration is even more true in the case of foreign policy. It is absolutely essential for any political association to appeal to violence and coercive measures both against foreigners and against adversaries within the country itself. Only this characteristic appeal to violence constitutes a political association within the meaning of our terminology. The state is an association, which claims a monopoly in the legitimate use of violence, and cannot be defined in any other way." Cf. Max Weber, *Essays in Sociology*, p. 334, as quoted by J. Milton Yinger, *Religion, Société, Personne*, Editions Universitaire, p. 270.

12. See *La Lettre*, No. 116, p. 19.

13. *Informations Catholiques Internationales*, No. 312, May 15, 1968, pp. 4-7.

14. M. Peuchmaurd, "Esquisse pour une théologie de la révolution," *Parole et Mission*, 39, October 15, 1967.

15. See the text of Mons. Helder Camara's interview in the issue of *I.C.I.* mentioned in note 13. See also, Ivan Illich, "Violence, a Mirror for Americans," *America*, New York, April 27, 1968, which is wholly dedicated to revolution in Latin America.

16. See *Informations Catholiques Internationales*, May 1, 1968.

17. See chapter 3.

Chapter 5. Christianity and the Socialist Revolution

1. *Reflections on the Revolution of Our Time*, p. 24, London, 1944.

2. "The Jewish Question," *MEGA* I, 1/1, p. 603.

3. GS 21.

4. GS 43.

5. GS 65.

6. *The Communist Manifesto,* 1848.

7. GS 11.

8. Spanish translation, Mexico, 1905, p. 649.

9. Introduction to an inquiry among young intellectuals: *Difficult Certitudes,* bearing the title *Debating Aloud.*

10. Miguel De Unamuno, *The Agony of Christianity,* tr. Kurt F. Reinhardt (New York: Frederick Unger Publishing Co., 1960).

11. *De l'anathème au dialogue,* Paris, 1965, p. 42 f.

12. GS 55.

13. *La filosofia dell'uomo,* Editori Reuniti, 1964.

14. Ibid.

Chapter 10. Violence or Nonviolence in the Transformation of Society

1. *Christianisme sociale,* Nos. 1-2, 1967.